LEA

"Lead & Follow comes at the perfect time, to bring the missing piece in the plethora of leadership models suggested for our world: that of mastering the complementary skill of followership. Sharna Fabiano presents leadership as a dance, emphasizing the role of not just the leader but also the follower, making room for all the dramatic beauty and flow as well as maneuvering and creative tension that shows up in the everyday challenges we face at work and in relationships. One of the most refreshing as well as practical takes on leadership that I have seen in a long time."

—Nilima Bhat
Co-author of *Shakti Leadership* and founder of the Shakti Mission and the Shakti Fellowship

"An aesthetic delight! Fabiano shows how to master the dual roles of co-creating at work and invites us into the beauty of the dance."

—Ginny Whitelaw
Author of *Resonate: Zen and the Way of Making a Difference*

"Connect, collaborate, co-create. It's such a beautiful frame of the work of leaders and followers. By using tango as a methodology, Sharna Fabiano masterfully advances the field and charts an exciting path forward for educators and practitioners alike."

—Scott Allen, PhD
Associate professor of management, Boler College of Business, John Carroll University, and host of *Phronesis: Practical Wisdom for Leaders Podcast*

"I have read most of the literature on followership so am always curious to see what a new entry adds to the field. Sharna Fabiano's *Lead and Follow* is weaving together four threads that create a unique fabric of great value: 1) the embodied experience of leading and following through dance; 2) the transference of wisdom so gained to the social dynamics present in all teams; 3) a sense from her coaching practice of what enables individuals to perceive their growth direction and strategies; 4) a compendium of exercises that transfer these benefits to a self-development toolkit. This book is a magnificent achievement wrapped in the empathy, warmth, clarity, and strength that the best teachers bring to those eager to learn."

> —Ira Chaleff
> Author of *The Courageous Follower: Standing Up To and For Our Leaders*

"Leadership and followership are inextricably connected, and there is no better metaphor for this interrelationship than the tango. Sharna Fabiano invites us into the world of social dance and into the true relationship between leading and following. Leaders (and team members) who understand this relationship will clearly have an advantage."

> —Ronald E. Riggio, PhD
> Henry R. Kravis professor of leadership and organizational Psychology, Claremont McKenna College

"Sharna offers a much-needed and invaluable look at the leader-follower dynamic with this guided journey through the lens of tango dance. As an organization development consultant, coach, storyteller, and scholar/practitioner of leadership and organization change, I resonated with this entire masterfully written piece of work."

> —Karen L. Gilliam, PhD
> Agency chief learning officer and organization development lead, NASA

"Poetic, innovative, and powerfully practical. This book inspires and instructs in how to leverage the subtle dance of leading and following that exists within each of us, no matter our job title or role. As graceful a writer as she is a dancer, Sharna masterfully articulates how the nuanced art of tango provides a potent metaphor for navigating fluid power relationships in today's modern workspace. If you are at all interested in cultivating higher levels of connection, collaboration, and creativity in your work, this is a must-read."

—Amy Lombardo
Author of *Brilliance* and founder of the Brilliance Academy for Personal Transformation and Social Change

"Instead of situating leadership in another board—or Zoom—room, Sharna offers a visceral method for understanding the complex relationship between leaders and followers through the metaphor of tango. Within the diverse organizations on our global dance floor, anyone practicing, studying, or teaching leadership will find tremendous value in the detailed skill pairings, exercises, and self-coaching techniques packed into this practical and accessible guidebook."

—Dan Jenkins, PhD
Associate professor of leadership and organizational studies, University of Southern Maine, co-author of *The Role of Leadership Educators: Transforming Learning*, and co-host of *The Leadership Educator Podcast*

"*Lead & Follow* is a passionate and compassionate book, organized in a way that makes it highly usable. Sharna immerses the reader in evocative descriptions of how one follows and leads well in the expressive dance of the tango. Then she gently and wisely guides us to see ourselves anew in the workplace in both of those roles."

—Marc Hurwitz and Samantha Hurwitz
Co-authors of *Leadership Is Half the Story: A Fresh Look at Followership, Leadership, and Collaboration*

"Sharna Fabiano's book is a joy to read! As a retired Air Force officer, program manager, and systems engineer in industry, and entrepreneur, I have read innumerable books on leadership. In my over forty years of professional life, I have never come across one that uses the metaphor of tango for followership and leadership. It is a welcome and fresh perspective on these two subjects. Sharna's advice on leadership connection, collaboration, and co-creation are spot on for what today's leaders need to do to succeed. If you are a leader, buy this book, internalize its recommendations, and apply what it says!"

—Frank DiBartolomeo
Speaker, presentation skills/interview skills coach, retired US Air Force lieutenant colonel, and author of *Speak Well and Prosper: Tips, Tools, and Techniques for Better Presentations*

"Sharna Fabiano remarkably translates the physical experience of tango improvisation into practical lessons everyone can benefit from. Most importantly, she highlights the unsung hero: the follower. The boldness of this book is very well grounded in the author's own expertise in tango, a dance form that is surprisingly radical by virtue of its interdependent roles. And by describing the interplay of leading and following, this book illuminates one of our most persistent blind spots around power dynamics."

—Valeria Solomonoff
Award-winning choreographer and tango professor at Tisch School of the Arts, New York University

"Improvisational social dancers are experts in leader/follower collaboration, and Fabiano (a master of both roles in tango) translates these skills for business contexts, boldly recognizing the undervalued skills of followership as an essential complement to leadership and offering a blueprint for developing both without ever stepping on a dance floor."

—Juliet McMains, PhD, professor of dance, University of Washington

"This book focuses on a place that many have not looked at, nor allowed themselves to feel. Reflecting her experience as both dancer and coach, Sharna points to the active participation of the follower. I risk saying that Sharna's objective in this book is revolutionary. If we read it carefully and understand it, we can change the way we relate socially, in dance, at work, and in all aspects of life."

—Jose Garofalo
Director of the Cambalache Festival of Tango, Theater, and Dance, and tango professor at the University of Buenos Aires

"Using her extensive experience dancing and teaching tango, Fabiano outlines three phases of coming together that produce team greatness—all from the perspective of the leader and, to an even greater extent, the often-overlooked follower. Throughout this practical book, concrete examples and metaphors clarify the benefits and impact of navigating each role exceptionally well. A must-read for team members, regardless of position."

—Christi Barrett
Coach and trainer at Humanergy, and co-author of *What Great Teams Do Great: How Ordinary People Accomplish the Extraordinary*

Lead and Follow:

The Dance of Inspired Teamwork

By Sharna Fabiano

© Copyright 2021 Sharna Fabiano

ISBN 978-1-64663-279-4

Published by

◤ köehlerbooks™

3705 Shore Drive
Virginia Beach, VA 23455
800−435−4811
www.koehlerbooks.com

LEAD

THE DANCE OF
INSPIRED TEAMWORK

& FOLLOW

SHARNA FABIANO

VIRGINIA BEACH
CAPE CHARLES

For the dancers

"To know oneself is to study oneself in action
with another person."
—Bruce Lee

TABLE OF CONTENTS

PREFACE

With great fondness I recall the friend who first piqued my interest in the tango through, of all things, scent. His cologne, W claimed, the name of which I promptly forgot, was the fragrance of Buenos Aires, 1943. We were chatting in a bar in between sets of swing music, and I glanced at him with an eyebrow raised. Without pausing for breath, he insisted I accompany him the very next evening to a *milonga,* or Argentine tango social dance. Then he left.

While the next twenty-four hours passed, I considered the extent of W's excitement at this invitation, which was considerable. I didn't know him very well, but we had common friends. And with his description of the tango—amazing, exquisite, beautiful, subtle—it was as if he were about to escort me to an enchanted realm that he alone had discovered. I felt certain I was about to experience something special, something magical.

This was back in October 1997, the tail end of the dot-com bubble. I had finished college earlier that year and taken a job in web development. Social dancing was my way of meeting people outside work. On this particular evening, a brisk fall breeze swept leaves around our feet as my friend hurried me down the sidewalk. Entering through the heavy, century-old side door of the First Baptist Church in Cambridge, Massachusetts, I took my first deep breath of the musical nostalgia that characterizes Argentine tango.

The violins and the *bandoneón*[1] wove their stories back and forth while eight or ten couples slowly but deliberately made their way around the dark hardwood floor, each mapping their own version of the dramatic narrative. One couple, for a moment, appeared totally still, until I spied the woman's stiletto heel slowly and carefully circling around the edge of her partner's shoe. Others whirled only a few feet from us, their bodies wrapped together, and then glided smoothly away, lost in their own world.

Who were these people? Were they lovers? Strangers? And the tall, unassuming man in a flannel shirt changing the CD? Everything seemed saturated with purpose, each step, each sudden dip of melody. How appropriate it was, in retrospect, to discover tango in a sacred space, a high-arched sanctuary converted to a large dance hall, where the aging wood beams and floorboards seemed to whisper old stories. There are spiritual roots in all dance traditions, and the tango assumes the role with a quiet intensity. Whatever this Argentine tango was, I wanted to know more.

Taking me aside, my date for the evening delivered my first lesson. Extending his arms and grinning ear to ear, he prompted encouragingly, "Give me a hug!" One of the hardest parts of partner dancing, at least for those who didn't grow up with it, is also one of the most essential—getting close. When I hugged W for the first time that evening, I noticed the softness of his black dress shirt, that it had a very subtle, checked texture to it, and that it was, of course, scented. "Good," he said, as I stepped into his arms. "Now, give me your right hand. Very good. Now we walk."

---

1   The *bandoneón* is a type of nineteenth-century German concertina. Originally designed to replace church organs, it later became a primary instrument in traditional tango orchestras in Argentina and Uruguay.

So much is conveyed in that layman's translation of tango. The embrace, they say, tells you everything before the first step is ever taken. This goes far beyond clothing and personal grooming. Getting close requires trust on the one hand and responsibility on the other. It requires a certain amount of self-confidence and the good kind of pride. Most of all, it implies risk.

I remember those first three seconds of tango as a blank slate. I had no idea what would happen, and fortunately I didn't have time to panic. Somehow we made it around the room together in that spontaneous embrace. I became one of those deliberate dancers, listening intently for some clue as to what was coming next. Later it was explained to me that the tango is an improvised dance, that you're not supposed to know, that you make things up as you go along. Of course, that's not the whole story, but it's one of tango's central narratives.

Over the next fifteen years, I dove headlong into that narrative, leaving my full-time job and stock options behind to work freelance so that I could travel to Buenos Aires again and again to study and dance tango. My tango journey also took me to New York, Amsterdam, Berlin, and many lesser-known destinations, both to train and also to simply dance all night long, absorbing the tango into my body memory.

Over time, I tried on nearly all the hats there are to wear as a member of the international, grassroots tango community: dancer, DJ, teacher, organizer, producer, performer, choreographer, publicist, small business owner, nonprofit director. The tango community unwittingly ushered me into adulthood, and social dancing, in many ways, helped me discover who I wanted to be in the world.

During this process, I gradually realized that I was becoming a more open and less guarded person because of the many, many other people I was dancing with. A textbook introvert, I became fascinated by how relationships were formed through the leading and following roles, how trust could be both built and destroyed by either side without uttering a single word, and how I could sincerely be myself with others while maintaining safe and ethical boundaries.

Among the most humbling lessons I learned from the tango is to see miscommunications rather than errors, to seek greater clarity rather than blaming a partner for taking the "wrong step." I saw again and again that when both partners focused on the task at hand, the "right and wrong" framework faded. Instead, it became evident that every dance is a conversation, bringing its own surprises, challenges, and thrills. The beauty of the tango, for me, is the amazing opportunity to create something new together in every dance.

I count myself blessed that my early teachers encouraged everyone to study both leading and following roles instead of assigning them by gender. Learning in this way gave me empathy and appreciation for my partners, and the freedom to dance with both men and women. I quickly discovered that leading was not entirely about being in charge, and that following was not entirely about giving up control. It was so much more complex than that. For me, social dance quickly grew beyond just entertainment; it became a wider experience of community and belonging.

The tango world, of course, has its fair share of discrimination and power plays, but I think dancing both roles actually helped me to screen out much of the negativity. I quickly got to know many more people than I otherwise would have, and dancing with so many different partners made me less attached to any one particular tango experience and more intrigued with the tango itself. I focused more and more on the subtlety of improvised communication achieved through a blend of technique and intention. I saw, and felt, how complementary leading and following roles could foster growth and creativity, and how lack of activation in one role, or willful dominance of one role over the other, immediately crippled that growth.

In 2016, I stepped back from the world of dance to become a professional coach. Whereas my former dance students had struggled with mixed signals and uncomfortable posture, my coaching clients now described dismissive supervisors, distracted colleagues, and anxiety over performance and approval. Breakdowns in communication were everywhere, in organizations large and small, just like they had been on the dance floor. But there was one key difference.

Dancers may struggle to harmonize with their partners, but they view their discomfort as temporary, something to be smoothed out through training. They have two specific methods of training available to them: leading skills development and following skills development. In the business world, though, the approach was fundamentally lopsided. Leadership training was prescribed as an answer to nearly every interpersonal problem, but there was a complete vacuum around the role of following. No one talked about following at all, except as something to avoid.

The social dancer in me couldn't help but find this strange, and wonder if the overemphasis on leadership might be a root cause of many internal business challenges. After all, in most business environments, the term *follower* is a synonym for *worthless*. Everyone is expected to be a leader, or to express leadership qualities. Taking that approach on the dance floor, I knew, was a recipe for disaster, or, at the very least, disappointment. Could a reframing of leadership and followership functions be part of the solution for struggling teams and organizations? Could a reclaimed vision of strong, influential following, alongside leading, transform what many thought possible in the realm of professional work?

This book is an exploration of those questions. Consider that two Spanish verbs frequently used for the terms *lead* and *follow*[2]— *marcar* and *responder*—translate more precisely as "show the way" and "respond." This is a process that takes place between two people when dancing the tango, but it's a principle that we can also use at

---

2   In many social dance cultures, including tango, gendered terms such as man's role and woman's role are considered historically accurate and are still used by some instructors today. Adoption of the terms lead and follow, however, has become widespread in recent decades.

work. There are moments when we show the way to someone else, whether we supervise others or not, and there are other times in which we respond to others who do the same for us. The *manner* in which we play either of these roles—say, with resentment or with generosity—determines both the experience and the output of every professional interaction.

The trick when translating tango principles into the work environment is in fully accepting that the one who leads, or shows the way, in any given moment is not superior or more valuable than the one who follows, or responds. Rather, it is the two choosing to operate together, in a complementary fashion, that makes things progress smoothly. The roles of leading and following may shift throughout the day or throughout the year, especially as the model of working in teams becomes the new standard. Leading and following actions may not even always correspond to official titles. But if we want everyone to demonstrate leadership qualities, we're going to need followership qualities as well.

In the corporate environment, it's tempting to understand our positions as a hierarchy of intrinsic value, rather than a hierarchy of functional accountability. If we want to nurture and strengthen the human potential of our workforce, we need to recognize that everyone's position is valuable, and interact with others in a way that reflects that belief. Defining both sides of the communication equation, leading and following, helps us to do that.

And when we commit to seeing equal value, we will be doing what the most innovative and influential social dancers do: bringing out the very best in one another. As a team, people can produce more than they can alone, but they can also make one another miserable and, out of that misery, cause failures of epic proportion. This book shares a method for building inspiring and creative relationships in order to produce inspiring and creative work. Its goal is to support exceptional teamwork. So often we prioritize work over relationship. What might we learn by reversing that order, and putting relationship first?

INTRODUCTION

*T*here are approximately ten feet between your chair and the edge of the dance floor. You are seated at a small café table, and the tall stranger, the leader, is standing calmly in front of you. Eye contact confirms your silent agreement to become partners for the next set of dances. This moment is sacred, a tiny pocket of time in which you both acknowledge that although you are individuals, you will now come together to play the roles of leader and follower, a creative team, interdependent. You do this because you know that you cannot dance alone, that you need a partner, or many partners, to make the dance happen. The paradox is that in prioritizing the relationship, you discover an unexpected sense of freedom, and you achieve more together than what is possible through individual effort alone.

There is something mysterious about each recognizing the need for the other that lifts both partners up and makes social dance greater than the sum of its parts. It's not just mechanical execution; it's synergy. The reciprocal nature of leading and following in social dance offers useful lessons for professional workplace interactions, although the term *follower* may be less familiar there. At work, too, there is power in recognizing that we can lift each other up, that we are each capable of more when we collaborate successfully together. The structure of improvised social dance offers an elegant, if unusual, framework for designing such collaboration.

The image of two dance partners coming together may initially seem romantic, but it is also a practical metaphor. The act of *choosing* is powerful in any situation, whether you're stepping into a dance embrace or a weekly meeting. It may be easy to forget that you choose to go to work every day just as much as your boss does, but you do. From that daily choice flow others: to complete reports, to respond to calls, to troubleshoot code. These actions may be listed in your job description or even labeled *required*, but on a practical level you still choose every day to perform them. When you remember this, you start to reclaim the strength of the followership role, which is only passive if you think it is. It's popular to think of everyone being a leader, because leadership is associated with power. But what if power could flow up as much as it flows down through the hierarchy of a company or department? Perhaps power can flow in all directions.

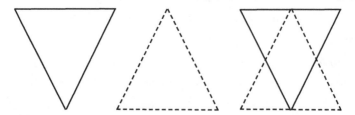

Conventional notions of hierarchy emphasize the expression of leadership, and suggest that power flows from the top down, as in the first triangle. But a second, invisible flow of power is available from below. This is the supportive role of followership, represented by the second triangle. The creative synergy of both roles together is represented by the diamond formed by the two overlapping triangles, when both downward and upward flows are activated.

While leadership is a much-celebrated subject in the professional world, followership is an idea rarely thought of at all, much less thought of as important. In our offices, institutions, and governments, the act of following has been eclipsed by an ardent focus on leading, perhaps because in those environments leaders interact with groups and teams, rather than as part of a simpler one-to-one partnership. One leader has many followers, whereas a follower has only one leader. Most work environments are also hierarchical structures, with leaders placed above groups of followers. And, inasmuch as the leader is traditionally a male figure, many employers also continue to value masculine qualities over feminine ones, even as more and more women assume leadership roles. Given these factors, it's easy to see how leadership has been strongly emphasized and followership overlooked.

In the social dance world, however, followership is harder to ignore. There are two partners, and each of them has a role. Decades ago, those roles were labeled *man* and *woman*, but today they are increasingly labeled *leader* and *follower* instead. Significantly, that change in vocabulary disconnects role from gender, and the increasingly common physical reality of women leading and men following on the dance floor has opened a rich inquiry into the nature of both roles.

Dancers have been asking themselves this for years: If roles are no longer defined by gender (leader/man, follower/woman), then how are they defined? What actions, gestures, qualities, and tasks might be learned so that any person might lead? So that any person might follow? Further, how do those tasks work together to enhance the creativity, efficiency, safety, and comfort of dancing? Throughout our culture, leadership skills are prized, though inconsistently defined. The duet form of social dance, however, makes *followership* conspicuous as a skill set as well. It is one of the primary areas of study in which this is true.

Dancers generally understand leading and following roles as complementary, not hierarchical, although a masculine, leader-centric bias does linger in many individual dance communities. Nevertheless, social dance reveals the influence we have on one another in real time, in the body, and so the articulation of roles in a dance context is considerably more equitable than it is in the average work environment. Because of their clear delineation of how collaboration skills are first learned and then put into practice, social dancers provide valuable insights for teams working in the business world, where following impacts our daily work every bit as much as leading does, even if it is less visible.

Strong followership, as dancers know it, is at once attentive, supportive, responsible, meticulous, and expressive. This kind of following can give employees a deep sense of purpose, bring out the best in managers and supervisors, and accelerate productivity. Exceptional following enables, stabilizes, and liberates those in official leadership roles to do their jobs better, and in some ways it can even influence the scope of those jobs.

Expert leading, of course, ensures accountability, timely decision-making, and forward motion, but sustaining a working community of people who consistently produce creative solutions requires something more. It requires a dynamic way of relating to one another that dancers refer to as *improvisation*. To a dancer, improvisation does not mean "winging it" or making it up as you go along. Rather, it implies a highly refined system of communication built through specific methods of training. Improvisation for dancers is a synergy between leading and following actions that is greater than the sum of its parts. We already know a lot about leading at work, but not many of us understand how to follow with intelligence, power, and grace, as dancers do. It's time we learned.

TANGO AS METHODOLOGY

Though trained in multiple forms of dance and movement, for twenty years I chose to study and work primarily within the global community of tango social dance. This world, in many ways, is the inverse of the commercial image typically associated with tango. Like many imported cultural traditions, tango has been wildly mischaracterized, distorted by sexualized stereotypes, sequins, and flashy moves. In fact, the community-based form of tango is a subtle, complex language built around organic pedestrian movement. It requires many years to master. Tango, the dance, lives alongside the equally sophisticated tradition of tango, the music, born in the Rio de la Plata, the port region of modern-day Buenos Aires, Argentina, and Montevideo, Uruguay.

Much like African-American jazz, tango music and dance emerged in the early twentieth century in the midst of economic hardship and racialized class conflict. Growing out of neighborhood gatherings in municipal centers and tenement courtyards—not on theater stages or in academic studios—social tango is a creative, participatory activity through which dancers escape the everyday to access, for a short time, experiences of wholeness, belonging, beauty, and joy. Regardless of your circumstances, it is possible to feel powerful, safe, accepted, even cherished, on the dance floor. In this way, tango is a democratic technique of transcendence made for the people by the people, and traditionally passed down in the manner of folk tradition, person to person, through families and close-knit social networks.

I began to study the tango tradition in the late 1990s, both in Buenos Aires and also in the many North American and European cities where it has been transplanted. In the course of my journey, I discovered profound lessons of interdependence embedded within its leading and following roles. Like the Chinese philosophical principle of yin and yang, every function of one partner corresponds to a complementary function of the other, and it is in this intricately woven dialogue that the creativity of tango develops, like jazz, with endless variations in timing, style, and expression.

Over the years, tango became much more than a dance for me. It became a practice through which I understood human potential, both as a relational exchange between two people and as an internal, left and right-brain discourse within the individual. My physical tango training of alternately leading and following in creative dialogue served as an unusual reference point when I later changed careers and became a life coach.

In the professional stories of my coaching clients, I began to hear the virtues of leadership extolled over and over again, while its invisible partner, followership, was omitted from the narrative. As a former tango dancer, this collective blind spot was striking. In discussions of career challenges, I saw leadership as half of a conversation waiting to be completed by its counterpart, followership. Yet, followership was like a ghost for most of my clients. Disparaged or erased, it was something they had no language for. Many were wary of it.

My social dance experience had proved to me that the *way* we work together really matters. In particular, tango showed me that the way a community or organization chooses to define *leader* and *follower* determines how individuals in that community behave when they stand in those roles. Dancing couples achieve artistic greatness or mediocrity, depending, in large part, on those definitions and resulting behaviors. Our first task in the workplace, then, must be to clarify those roles. In particular, we must rewrite the *following* role in a positive light, as a position of strength.

Tango is a living embodiment of the creative leadership-and-followership dynamic, and because communication is physicalized in the act of dancing, the body instantly reveals when the team is malfunctioning. Not so obvious are breakdowns of communication in our places of work. The framework offered in this book translates the physical dialogue of tango into the less tangible realm of professional interaction so that complementary leading and following become visible, nameable skills and behaviors.

Crucial to the project of reclaiming followership as a powerful partner to leadership is the realization that the roles themselves need not be explicitly tied to title or position. That is, all members of an organization can act as both great leaders and great followers, and in fact benefit tremendously from doing so. Consider a middle manager who generally takes the leading role in relation to her direct reports, and then switches into the following role when meeting with her own supervisor. Similarly, entry-level employees may see themselves initially as followers, but may soon be encouraged to lead specific meetings or act as leaders on certain projects in their area of specialization.

All successful teams demonstrate what dancers would call a healthy lead-and-follow dynamic, even if the team members themselves do not describe their interactions in those terms. But because we lack language and understanding around *followership*, there isn't much of a road map to successful collaboration, and so not every team achieves it. This book is one such map. It can guide you in the direction of more authentic professional relationships and better work. At present, many companies encourage leadership training throughout their organizations. I propose that universal followership training be implemented as well, and just as rigorously. If everyone is going to lead, then everyone must also follow.

THE CASE FOR FOLLOWERSHIP

My life as a social dancer showed me that superior work—not to mention the most satisfying work—comes *not* from everyone leading all the time, but from leaders and followers working together. Even if dancers change roles throughout the evening, or within a single dance, the roles themselves must remain intact because they each represent distinct and complementary functions. Leading, no matter how skillful, does not remove the need for following, and neither does extraordinary following remove the need for leading.

Due to its negative connotation, some contemporary business thinkers avoid the term *follower* entirely, instead using terms such as *team player, individual contributor,* or even *tribe member.* However useful team structures may be, simply having them is not enough to nurture collaboration. And the typical focus on how to lead teams, rather than on the interpersonal dynamics of teamwork itself, overlooks the nuance of leader-follower interaction.

And so, by examining the social dance duet, we learn how the interplay of leading and following elevates human capacity in a way that is simply unachievable by other means. In *Powers of Two,* Joshua Wolf Shenk writes, "The pair is the primary creative unit."[3] Shenk debunks the myth of the lone genius with fascinating accounts of dozens of well-known creative pairs, and how they worked their magic. Even in cases of pairs featuring absent, hidden, or imaginary partners, it's clear that creative achievements flow from the relationship dynamic itself, not from one individual or the other.

With a nod to the tango, Shenk also makes this observation of the hierarchical power relationships commonly found in organizations.

> While it's usually clear who has the upper hand in creative pairs, the leader-follower schism can't be absolute. This is the paradox of power dynamics, and it's not easy to summarize. Put one way, it sounds like a contradiction: *High-level creative exchange depends on both hierarchical and fluid power relationships.* Put another way, it sounds like a truism: *To be a strong pair, both members must be able to lead and follow.*[4]

Organizational hierarchies are indeed useful, but we tend to exaggerate the importance of leadership. We need to understand that everyone in the organizational chart, regardless of their title, is also a follower.

---

3   Shenk, *Powers of Two,* xxii.

4   Shenk, *Powers of Two,* 175.

Many organizations skirt this issue by encouraging employees to *manage up*, or *lead from where they are* in the organizational structure. On the opposite side of the spectrum, the concepts of *flat*, *leaderless*, or *self-managed* organizations decentralize authority across a network or organization. These and other experimental structures rightly seek to adjust the circulation of power. There is a growing sense that conventional top-down flow is both culturally unsatisfying and practically insufficient. The more urgent the need for social change and technological innovation, the more obvious it becomes that the current system is not working. The concept of followership adds depth to the discussion of working together by proposing that two complementary roles might coexist in any given conversation, each enhancing the other's contribution while still honoring existing hierarchies of accountability.

In most workplaces, there is still a tendency to attribute all desirable behaviors to leadership and all undesirable behaviors to followership. The bias toward leadership is evident in the fact that so many managers and supervisors are held responsible for others' performance. This practice has become so normalized that we take it as given. But doesn't it make more sense for everyone to be responsible for their own performance? What effect does it have to assign responsibility elsewhere? The solution is not always more leadership. When we identify, instead, complementary behaviors for both leading and following, *desirable* becomes not one set of things but two. Not only the manager but also the team member is integral to success. By describing two skill sets, we paint a more realistic portrait of how we work together, and we make professional relationship skills more comprehensible and learnable.

A situation in which everyone is truly leading all the time is counterproductive. Just imagine a meeting in which twenty people are pitching ideas simultaneously. In order for one or some of us to lead, others must follow. In healthy organizations, people intuitively understand that they must alternate between these roles to some extent, even if they do not name them as such. In *The End of Leadership*, leadership scholar Barbara Kellerman traces recent historical shifts in how leadership and followership have been defined and understood. Her critique points out that the contemporary leadership industry's fixation on the role of the leader alone lags considerably behind social and political movements of the last half century:

> To the degree the industry remains focused, laser-like, on the leader, it is doing a disservice to itself and to those who pay good money to learn how to lead. . . . At a moment in history when . . . so many followers are not in the least inclined actually to follow the traditional view of "the leader," the suggestion that "the leader" is all-important is simply passé.[5]

Kellerman suggests that as *information, connectivity,* and *expressiveness*[6] in our world increase, followers will be heard, one way or another, and the leadership community will be forced to peer into its blind spot. When they do that, they may discover what is patently obvious to the social dancer: that the recognition and practice of both leading and and following roles is necessary for success. Many individual dancers who study both roles report increased levels of empathy, cohesion, joy, and innovation. They are strong communicators and inventive performers, and much like social entrepreneurs, they are often among the most influential and forward-thinking members of their communities, if not always the most popular.

An office community is a matrix of one-to-one relationships, overlapping and interwoven to form either a flexible, robust structure or a tangled ball of string—or, more likely, something in between.

---

5   Kellerman, *The End of Leadership*, 65.

6   Kellerman claims that leaders' power has decreased as technology has increased our access to information, our ability to connect with one another around it, and our confidence in expressing our views publicly.

The interpersonal dynamics running through this matrix of pairings determine its overall level of integrity. Think of the engineer who responds defensively to constructive feedback, or the manager who disregards the concerns of her sales reps. Negative human interactions ripple through organizations and quickly erode trust and productivity elsewhere. What if these breakdowns in communication are not inevitable, but rather represent underdeveloped following skills? Or an absence of balanced leader-follower relationship models?

Google's frequently referenced Project Aristotle[7] revealed that the most effective teams are not necessarily made up of the best and brightest minds, but rather of those minds (and hearts, perhaps) that demonstrate emotional intelligence and inclusivity. Similarly, leadership scholar Amy Edmonson identifies *psychological safety* as a key indicator of successful teamwork, or what she calls *teaming*. In *The Fearless Organization*, she defines psychological safety as "a climate in which people feel comfortable expressing and being themselves."[8]

She continues, "When people have psychological safety at work, they feel comfortable sharing concerns and mistakes without fear of embarrassment or retribution. They are confident that they can speak up and won't be humiliated, ignored, or blamed. They know they can ask questions when they are unsure about something." Importantly, Edmonson's concept of teaming extends beyond formal teams of people, instead referring to the interpersonal ability to work well in small groups no matter how temporary they may be, particularly in environments characterized by uncertainty and ambiguity. These findings are consistent with how social dancers describe healthy leader-follower connections. Dancers train to collaborate with multiple partners—often strangers—all with the perspective that there are no wrong steps and that the pair can *improvise* their way

---

7   Project Aristotle gathered and assessed data from 180 Google teams between 2012 and 2014 in an attempt to identify the characteristics of an ideal team.

8   Edmonson, *The Fearless Organization*, xvi.

out of any tight spots. Edmondson's research across a wide variety of industries demonstrates that strong interpersonal skills establish this kind of all-inclusive psychological safety, which in turn gives rise to high performance and innovation, just like it does on the dance floor.

By clearly naming not only what constitutes effective leadership but also what constitutes effective followership in the workplace, we expand the ways in which we can analyze, teach, and learn the interpersonal skills that produce reliable and consistent collaboration. Recognizing followership as a distinct skill set affirms intrinsic value for all members of a group. It helps us to reimagine work as an activity that can serve and sustain both our own individual needs and those of our team, company, school, community, or country. It doesn't have to be one or the other. We can have both.

A CHANGING WORKPLACE

Massive changes are currently in process as we establish higher levels of equity and inclusion in the workplace, and as the distinctions between for-profit and nonprofit missions begin to blur with the rise of socially conscious businesses and the "triple bottom line." The array of new knowledges and perspectives in the professional realm, combined with the flexibility of remote work, promises to enhance our capacity to innovate and problem-solve, but can create uncertainty in the short term.

Change at this scale requires that we deepen our understanding of how relationship impacts work. Two current models are the Agile Coaching Institute's team-driven work process and the lean startup[9] concept of entrepreneurship, which emphasizes a back-and-forth between developers and their target customers through rapid prototyping and iteration. Notably, the general idea of *soft*

9   Eric Ries's book *The Lean Startup* proposes a "build-measure-learn" feedback loop.

skills or *people skills*—distinct from technical or job-specific *hard skills*—is rapidly making its way to center stage as both a hiring criterion and a primary indicator of growth potential. The concept of followership is an important piece of the puzzle in this moment of cultural transformation. If we want to *create* a more balanced, equitable, sustainable world, we have to *be* more balanced, equitable, sustainable people. Seeing ourselves as both leaders and followers is an effective way to expand our collective potential.

Organizational consultants Marc and Samantha Hurwitz describe how the shift to working in teams, combined with an increasing reliance on interpersonal skills, points us toward the need for a robust leadership-followership dynamic. In *Leadership Is Half the Story*, they write,

> What makes a partnership or team truly engaged, productive, and creative? Research stresses this: everyone on the team is equally important in getting the job done AND is viewed and treated that way. Essentially, followership must be an equal partner to leadership. It sounds simple. But it only works when the roles of leadership and followership are acknowledged, understood, and optimized.[10]

The Hurwitzes' organizational development model, *generative partnership,* includes a system of five matching pairs of skills, one set for leadership and one for followership. The parallel structure of their curriculum underscores the pressing need to fill in the gaps around the followership role as a means of ensuring the health and sustainability of whole teams and companies.

In fact, the terms *leader* and *follower* are best understood not as fixed professional titles, but as strategic and empowering ways of relating to one another. In his seminal work, *The Courageous*

---

10   Hurwitz, *Leadership is Half the Story*, 8.

Follower, thought leader Ira Chaleff writes, "Most of us are leaders in some situations and followers in others. . . . They are two sides of one process, two parts of a whole. Teachers and students form a learning circle around a body of knowledge or skills; leaders and followers form an action circle around a common purpose."[11]

Each position, with its respective skill set, aligns with the other as a lock with its proverbial key. Both must come together to open the door. The alignment may be temporary, lasting only as long as a single interview or group meeting, or it may be ongoing, as in full-time employment or long-term community undertakings. The positions shift based on context, and on the requirements of the team's purpose. Chaleff continues, speaking both to the resistance that lingers around the followership role and to the tremendous opportunity waiting on the other side:

> There seems to exist the deepest discomfort with the term *follower*. It conjures up images of docility, conformity, weakness, and failure to excel. Often, none of this is the least bit true. The sooner we move beyond these images and get comfortable with the idea of *powerful* followers supporting *powerful* leaders, the sooner we can fully develop and test models for dynamic, self-responsible, synergistic relationships in our organizations.[12]

Social dancers know that if both partners try to lead, the couple doesn't get anywhere. So often, however, that is what happens in our workplaces. As leadership alone is celebrated, an excess of initiative and direction—without enough support and grounding—results in conflict, disconnect, and loss. The follower's balance, poise, and precision, as well as his or her willingness to trust, wait, and engage persuasively when necessary, largely determine the success or failure

---

11   Chaleff, *The Courageous Follower*, 2.

12   Chaleff, *The Courageous Follower*, 3.

of any partnership. Teams and companies that value followership qualities like close listening, thoughtful questioning, and the setting of healthy boundaries are the ones building sustainable futures today.

REDEFINING LEADERSHIP AND FOLLOWERSHIP

If the value of leadership still seems more obvious than that of followership, it may be at least partly because we often take followership skills for granted, including the deceptively complex ability to get work done, and to get it done well and on time. Unlike leadership training for managers and executives, companies rarely invest in corresponding followership training for their employees, yet they are frequently disappointed when these "invisible" skills are absent.

Ironically, the response is often to invest in even more leadership training for managers, reasoning that better leaders will make followers better. This strategy may be partially successful, but what if the opposite were also true? What if effective followers could actually make leaders more effective? Perhaps if we begin to name and articulate the impact of followership skills, investment and training in them will become just as critical as investment and training in leadership skills.

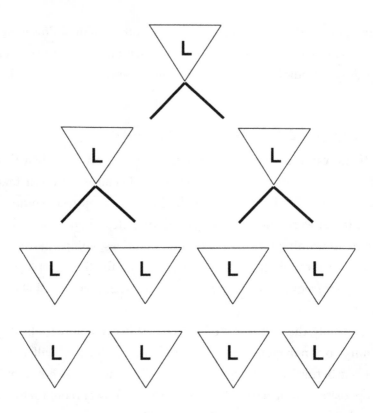

If our organizations were made up of exclusively leaders, this would be the ideal organizational chart. But if everyone is a leader, who is following those leaders?

It's worth noting that despite the term *follower* still being rather cringeworthy in many contexts, the truth is that if there are leaders, there are obviously other employees who follow those leaders, and in a hierarchical organization, there are many levels of leaders who nonetheless follow someone else above them. Structurally speaking, then, even though leading is emphasized (managing, supervising, directing), it's true that everyone in the organization also plays the role of the follower, at least some of the time. Even founders or CEOs are accountable to a board of directors, shareholders, customers, or the public. Why don't we acknowledge that fact, or consider it significant?

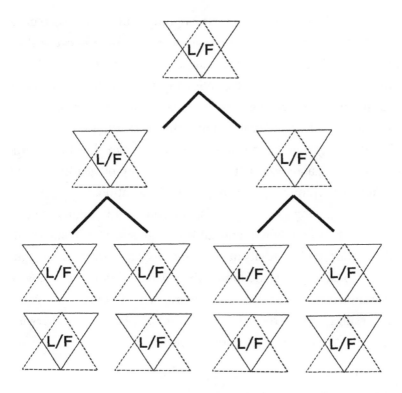

In a more integrated model of communication, every member of an organization is both leading and following, as the situation requires.

As more and more work happens in teams that are hierarchically flat, identifying leading and following dynamics can be subtle, yet no less important. Rather than labeling individuals *leaders* or *followers*, it may make more sense to understand behaviors as *leading* or *following*. For example, proposing ideas is an essential leading skill, with carefully listening and responding to those proposals being the following equivalent. Organizing a meeting efficiently is a necessary leading task. Complementary following actions include arriving to the meeting prepared and maintaining focus on its agenda. Often unnoticed, following skills nevertheless have tangible impact once we start tracking them.

The need for collaboration is ongoing, but many companies struggle to make it happen or sustain it over time because they fail to recognize, train, and track all relevant competencies. When combined with leading skills, following skills make teams more accurate, more discerning, and more stable amidst the uncertain realities that all organizations face. Understanding how the two roles work together, or fail to work together, can elevate a team's performance capacity. It is this integrated way of relating to one another that optimizes performance and innovation.

By recognizing following skills alongside leading skills, we can ensure strong accountability and cultivate higher levels of connection, collaboration, and creativity in our work. In order to do that, though, we need to take a good hard look at the old assumptions about power and authority that still linger in our workplaces. Often unconscious, these assumptions nevertheless compromise what might otherwise be energizing professional relationships.

LEARNING TO BOTH LEAD AND FOLLOW

Dancers characterize leadership by the capacity to invite or initiate skillfully. Actions that begin projects, launch campaigns, or start discussions are examples of this primary leading impulse. Beginning with the invitation to dance, leaders encourage action, and followers respond to that invitation by showing up with their full toolkit of resources ready to go. Indeed, following in the dance world is characterized primarily by responsiveness, and by a willingness to provide support, or to be *on board*.

In navigating the dance floor safely, the leader is focused on the big picture, not exclusively on the one-to-one relationship with each partner. Rather, the partner, the other couples on the dance floor, the musical arrangement, and many other environmental factors are all components in the leader's big-picture view. No matter what our title or position, if we are looking at the big picture, we are looking through the eyes of leadership. It is important that we all take this view from time to time, not only for the benefit of our current teams, but also as we lead ourselves along in our own careers.

Effective followers, by contrast, largely limit their focus to the tight circle of their one-to-one dance partnership. They are in the moment, crafting one step at a time, literally, with a demanding technique of balance, speed, precision, and expressiveness. At work, followership is a commitment to content, process, and quality. When we stand in the position of follower, we live in the details. Rather than the *big* picture, followership represents the *small* picture. It sees everyday tasks and individual relationships in fine grain. The followership view is deep where the leadership view is wide.

Think of the soldier in the field sending a combat report back to central command, or a factory worker alerting the foreman of a machinery breakdown. How about an airplane pilot and ground control? Or a senator and a citizen? No one person can hold both leading and following perspectives simultaneously, but both are essential. Following with strength and grace enables leaders to do their best work as much as the reverse.

To have the capacity for both deep and wide views is the path of integrated leader-followership, and we ought to all strive for that while at the same time recognizing our current sphere of influence and our position relative to others. We cannot all lead and follow at the same time, and so we must know when it is appropriate to fulfill each role. The better we are at both, the more easily we know when and how to switch, even on a moment-to-moment basis.

When two dancers come together representing these equally valuable, if distinct, expressions of power, they develop partnerships that move through three phases of increasing sophistication: *connection, collaboration*, and *co-creation*. In the workplace, these phases can provide scaffolding for effective teamwork, either in the space of a single meeting or on the scale of a multi-year project. In both dance partnerships and professional teams, the phases are cyclical, and deepen over time. Let's look a little bit closer at each one:

Connection: When beginner dancers learn to improvise together, their first task is to connect with a partner. Without the ability to connect, they literally cannot move together from their starting point, much less around the entire dance floor. Connection is partly a physical touch, and partly an attitude or intention. Think of a warm handshake. Now think of a weak, overpowering, or distracted one. In all scenarios, the hands touch, but the actual experience is greatly influenced by the intention behind that touch.

Dance connection is similarly an integration of action and intent, involving not only the hands but the arms and torso as well, and sometimes even the legs and feet. In learning to connect, followers primarily focus on what they do as an act of continuous *support* to the leader. How does the touch, posture, and placement of the body convey support and willingness? To answer this question, followers cultivate strong active-listening skills, awareness of their own movement, and sensitivity to the movements of their partners. In the way that they connect, followers must convey to the leader that they are ready and willing to be led, which means they trust the leader and commit to working together.

Leaders in social dance typically learn connection by focusing on *protecting* their partners, and are therefore focused on a different question: What will convey safety and comfort, and what will invite an enthusiastic response? Leaders ask followers to dance, and then they ask followers to do thousands of others actions throughout the duration of that dance. These requests must be protected in the sense that they must feel like things that the follower *wants* to do, or at minimum *can* do comfortably. In the way that they connect, leaders must convey to followers that they are able to lead responsibly—that is, able to make safe and desirable requests.

The concept of *rapport* is familiar in most work environments, but true connection goes deeper than superficial gestures and small talk. It's not enough to say the words or go through the motions. To lay a foundation for great teamwork, whatever we say or do must be accompanied by a clear intention to acknowledge and respect others on a human level. These acts of connection need not take a lot of time, but they do need to be sincere.

Collaboration: Once connected, dancers can then invent the spontaneous design of the movement in real time. To be good collaborators, followers must be prepared to execute any combination or timing that the leader assembles. They therefore focus their initial training on technical movement skills, including the capacity for both long, controlled, silent steps and short, playful ones, and everything in between. They become very good at balancing on the ball of one foot, and at spiraling and twisting through the center of the body. These concrete abilities make followers both calm and collected, and at the same time nimble and responsive.

In contrast, leaders learn specific dance vocabulary and how to combine multiple elements together into logical, aesthetic sequences. Further, they learn to arrange this dance material in time with musical rhythm and phrasing, all while navigating a crowded dance floor. In this phase, leaders accumulate a repertory of elements and combinations that they can execute consistently on a crowded dance floor with many different partners. They also familiarize themselves with dozens, if not hundreds, of tango songs that make up the canon of social dance music.

At work, the function of established systems or procedures can support healthy collaboration, but those elements are not collaboration in and of themselves. When we're collaborating effectively, there's a sense that we're discovering something together, that the work is evolving in a way that's not entirely predictable. We have guidelines and benchmarks, requirements even, but as we work together we need to always stay open to what the other person might suggest or produce, and what we might then be able to offer in return.

Co-creation: Improvising dancers who have mastered both material and technique begin to turn their attention to the artistry of what they are doing. After logging many, many miles on the dance floor, they make the form their own. Couples who dance together for years achieve a style of moving that no two others can reproduce. Excellence in social dance is not achieved by comparing oneself with others but rather by investing oneself in the dancing. A dancer becomes distinct from, not better than, others. All can therefore reach excellence in their own ways.

In the following role, this phase is about exploring aesthetic range and quality of movement. Dancers begin to express personality and style through movement. New and unusual flourishes and decorative elements emerge spontaneously. On the leader side, the exceptional improviser develops a kind of intuitive vision as the dance unfolds. This doesn't mean planning ahead, but rather that intimate knowledge of both musical arrangements and dance material allows for a flow of precise and complex decisions, each one informed by the last.

The ultimate goal of most projects is a creative one. Teams are tasked with solving a specific problem, or innovating to create change, improvement, or breakthrough. Difficult to plan, creative work is the natural outgrowth of steady collaboration. When teams are working well together, they inspire individuals to grow personally and professionally and generate the conditions for original thinking.

STRUCTURE OF THE BOOK

Like dancers, working professionals cycle through the three phases of relational skill-building over and over again: connect, collaborate, co-create, repeat. When all three phases are activated, working with others feels dynamic and productive, regardless of individual contributors' positions or areas of expertise. And like dancers, working professionals who practice both roles become more versatile and resilient than those who focus on only one.

Working through these relational phases in order, I identify nine leadership/followership skill pairs that parallel the training experiences of social dancers. Skills that establish clear *connection* with others are the ones that then allow us to *collaborate* effectively with them. In turn, once we can collaborate smoothly, relationships become more *co-creative* in nature. Just as we learn to walk before we run, and run before we fly, powerful relationships require a strong foundation to reach their full potential.

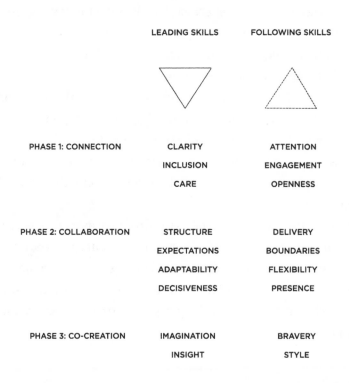

	LEADING SKILLS	FOLLOWING SKILLS
PHASE 1: CONNECTION	CLARITY	ATTENTION
	INCLUSION	ENGAGEMENT
	CARE	OPENNESS
PHASE 2: COLLABORATION	STRUCTURE	DELIVERY
	EXPECTATIONS	BOUNDARIES
	ADAPTABILITY	FLEXIBILITY
	DECISIVENESS	PRESENCE
PHASE 3: CO-CREATION	IMAGINATION	BRAVERY
	INSIGHT	STYLE

Because there is currently a deficit of material on the subject, I intentionally chose to delve more deeply into the followership side of working together than the leadership side. Each chapter therefore summarizes its relevant leadership skill only briefly, and then explores the corresponding following skill in greater detail, offering suggestions for practical application in the workplace. Like dance partners, leadership and followership continually influence one another. As two sides of the same coin, they never truly exist on their own. Two aspects of a relational phenomenon, each has the potential to hold the other back or elevate the other's efforts.

Because the context of our work is always changing, there is no one best way to approach either leading or following, and a perfect balance between the two is challenging to achieve. Nevertheless, the mutual desire to share power will always result in better outcomes. At work as in dance, following is more rewarding with a skilled leader, and leading is more successful with skilled followers. You may recognize some of the skills in this book as obvious or common sense, but others might be new or surprising. All are relevant for everyone, regardless of title or position.

At the end of the book, you'll find a journal with questions to help you track your learning from chapter to chapter as you experiment with harmonizing leadership and followership in your own professional interactions. You can use this journal on your own or as an anchor for group discussion when working with the material as part of a team.

Ultimately, the goal of this book is to encourage more productive dialogue in any environment where groups engage around a common purpose. The method presented here is offered as a means of deepening the conversation around what it means to work together, and to help make working together smarter, better, and more inspiring.

BEFORE WE BEGIN

Leadership and followership are two aspects of a relational phenomenon. They occur simultaneously, and cannot truly be separated. I have described them separately in this book for the purposes of understanding interpersonal dynamics more deeply. In our lived experience, however, *leading and following* is an ongoing, dynamic process. Dancers use the single term *improvisation* to refer to this process.

Because they are inspired by tango social dance, the definitions of leading and following described in this book may seem different from those you are familiar with. I invite you to experiment with what feels relevant to you and leave the rest. Here are a couple of points to consider about working with the material itself:

Although it is possible to make real changes in how you personally interact with others in your workplace, a more noticeable shift will occur when whole groups or teams practice the same set of guidelines. Share this material or the ideas in it with your coworkers or your manager.

Make small changes in low-stakes situations, working your way up to higher-stakes scenarios.

The three phases build on one another, and are also cyclical. If a relationship is strained, focus on connection skills. You may be surprised by how frequently they are overlooked, and by how powerful they are when used intentionally.

Professional growth requires both inner work (reflection, inquiry, and mindset) and outer work (speech and action). Use this book as a resource rather than as a formula, and choose a combination of internal and external practices that are relevant to your current challenges and to your specific work environment.

You may notice that some of the skills named in this book seem to contradict one another. This is because relationships are dynamic and need different adjustments at different times in order to stay healthy. Just as they are on the dance floor, every relationship you form at work is unique, and will evolve with the natural flow of changing circumstances. Working with others is an ongoing learning process.

Social dancers value their dance-community relationships just as much as, and sometimes more than, their actual dance experiences. This is a surprising yet powerful perspective to take into the work environment, where we tend to see relationship-building as just another strategy for professional success, not as a worthwhile goal in and of itself. Although it may seem counterintuitive at first, try prioritizing the human relationships you have with others over your concern for the work itself, and see how both are altered as a result.

Each chapter includes a short section titled "The follower's view from the dance floor." In these descriptions of real-time dance movement, the pronouns used for both leader and follower are she/her/hers. This choice works to challenge the male leader/female follower convention and normalize the idea that leadership and followership are gender-neutral roles wherever they are performed, on or off the dance floor.

The practices and strategies offered in this book are not intended to address any diagnosed educational or mental health conditions, nor incidents of discrimination or abuse. Please seek additional support and guidance from your personal and professional community as needed.

PART I:

CONNECTION

"Leadership is setting the frame.
Followership is creating within it."
—Marc and Samantha Hurwitz

LEADING SKILLS   **FOLLOWING SKILLS**

CLARITY   **ATTENTION**

INCLUSION   **ENGAGEMENT**

CARE   **OPENNESS**

Social dancers spend a significant portion of their early training cultivating the ability to connect. They explore, in minute detail, various sensations of touch and pressure in the arms and torso, and learn to shift their body weight from one foot to the other in tandem—without speaking. But the specifics of the physical connection differ for every pair of dancers because every individual body is unique. For this reason, tango postures and techniques vary widely. Ultimately, the best shape or arm placement is the one that creates the clearest feeling of connection for the couple. Without this clear feeling of togetherness, movement feels awkward, and the available vocabulary of steps remains limited.

Along with spatial directions like left, right, and stop, dancers learn to deliberately transmit attitudes such as trust, reliability, enthusiasm, confidence, and support to one another through their physical connection. Regardless of style or musical interpretation, a successful dance connection is one in which many layers of information flow back and forth, replacing the perception of two with the awareness of one.

We don't always think about what we project to others through our posture or our walk, as dancers do, but it's still true that how we hold ourselves, both physically and mentally, makes a difference. As dancers move together, they adjust their shape as needed to keep the channel of communication open, allowing every step to serve their common goal. Professional interactions, too, can shift from moment to moment, or over longer periods of time, in order to maintain a clear and supportive connection.

One way our work becomes meaningful, not to mention more productive, is by strengthening our relationships with others. Connection, in this sense, is a feeling of mutual investment in a shared purpose. We want to know that others can be trusted and relied upon to pursue this purpose alongside us, for mutual benefit. It's not enough to write these things into a mission statement or paint them on the wall of the office. The physical body must register a felt sense of connection for it to matter. How do we make sure that happens?

Your work may not bring you into physical contact with others, but your verbal and nonverbal connections with coworkers, clients, managers, vendors, contractors, students, investors, or the public can nevertheless establish a sense of mutual commitment and connection—what dancers call *moving as one*. All members of a team, of course, must come together to create this sense of connection, but they do so in different ways.

Leadership involves connecting with multiple individuals, groups, institutions, industries, and other entities. Leaders have the challenge of maintaining all of these connections over time without unfairly or unjustly privileging some over others. The more complex and extensive the network, the greater the power and impact of the leadership role. Followership, in contrast, is generally expressed by connecting with one person at a time. It can look like listening, supporting, asking questions, taking interest in what others have to say, and validating their presence and contribution.

What has been termed *emotional labor* falls largely into the category of connection: the continuous nurturing of interpersonal relationships in any team environment. Often unseen, this aspect of both leadership and followership is essential to the proper functioning of any group or network, no matter how vast. Though rarely recognized or compensated, it is the invisible human touch that holds us together. When we all learn to connect with one another from both the leader and follower position, the organizational culture becomes more stable and healthy.

Part I describes how team members can build connection with three matching pairs of leadership and followership skills: clarity/attention, inclusion/engagement, and care/openness. Even if you hold a formal leadership title in your work environment, consider under what circumstances you may also follow others in your team or organization.

Questions to Get Started
1. *What does connection mean to me?*
2. *What benefit does feeling connected bring to me, my work, and my team?*
3. *What do I perceive as my primary obstacle to connecting with others at work?*

CHAPTER 1:
CLARITY AND ATTENTION

CLARITY
+
ATTENTION
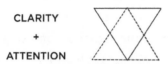

The Leader's Role: Communicate clearly

Looks Like: Expressing relevant information, objectives, goals, and instructions understandably and concisely; transparency; eye contact; positive tone of voice

Benefit: Keeps work moving along on schedule; reduces the frequency of delays, errors, and conflicts; provides focus; sets priorities

Impact: Helps others to do their work well

When It's Missing: Confusing or contradictory information, vague or indirect phrasing, excessive narration

---

Just like at work, good teamwork on the dance floor begins with clear communication. Tango dancers train the body to rest in equilibrium by relaxing muscle groups that are not needed while engaging others that are. Their movements are centered, minimal, and efficient, much like martial artists. In the leading role, this physical training contributes to clear thinking and precise communication. Even though dancers communicate through nonverbal signals rather than spoken language, their training in physical awareness is one powerful insight that applies directly to the work environment. We can take everyday moments of mental struggle as a cue to reconnect with our bodies with simple stretching, a short walk, or deep breathing. Very often, the return to an embodied sense of self clears the mind.

Experienced leaders on the dance floor usually know when they are *not* expressing themselves clearly, because following partners train themselves to wait for a signal before they take each step. If there is no signal, or if the signal is confusing, the follower—and therefore the couple—remains still until the message is repeated or clarified. A return to physical awareness is built in. At work, leader-follower misunderstandings are not this tangible, but we can still learn to identify them. Imagine feeling frustrated during a long meeting, or working hard to describe a proposal yet still sensing that no one is really getting it. Have you watched as team members nod in silence and then move on, forgetting what immediately came before? As described later in this chapter, follower training includes active listening and the asking of specific questions—complementary skills that help the leader stay clear. Without this supportive feedback loop, we might assume others are with us when they are not.

Indeed, beginner dancers in the following role sometimes go on autopilot, assuming they know what to do even when they haven't heard what the leader is asking for. Or they may invent something on their own, disregarding the leader's direction completely. When this happens, the couple's dancing is choppy and erratic. At work, comparable communication breakdowns aggravated by passive follower behavior can result in missed opportunities, delay, redundancy, conflict, or error. It's part of the leader's role to notice when communication isn't getting through. If we pause in these moments, as dancing leaders might, we can save time, reconnect with the group, and then move forward together.

Whether leading a single meeting or as a primary job description, we encourage attentive listening and engagement from team members by communicating in clear, concise language. Everyone needs this skill, of course, whether leading or following, but when we act from a position of leadership, we need it *more urgently*. Goals and tasks must be clear in order for teams to function. Information must be transparent if others are to make responsible decisions. A single leader can perform this function, or a team may clarify plans for itself collectively, sharing the leadership role.

Dancers use a repertory of physical movement signals to communicate, and learn quickly that the signal that works with one partner doesn't always work with another. They therefore train to notice when followers are not responding, when they don't understand, or when they've misunderstood, and to adjust the tone and intensity of their body language accordingly. Professionals use words in place of movements, but they must develop the same versatility in their abilities to speak and write. Team members who do not understand what is being asked of them will struggle to complete their work, no matter how skilled in their craft. To lead a variety of other people, we must have a variety of ways of expressing ourselves in language.

P, a real estate development specialist, told me about two very different experiences with two very different supervisors. When he was first hired at his current job, he reported to the director of his department, and right away, there were problems. The director's mood was unpredictable, and he regularly interrupted P or cut him off mid-sentence. In an early meeting, P recalls, "The director checked his cell phone, swiveled and checked his email, responded to emails, then would suddenly interject, 'What about x? Has he done x?' when the project supervisor and I had just discussed x. Then he would go back to checking his cell phone, sending a text, and checking email."

Because the director refused to communicate with him directly, P was never sure what he wanted. Worried about losing his job, P began working late and on weekends to do extra research, and took on parts of a coworker's project in an attempt to please the director. But even when others asked P to provide specific information in meetings, the director still ignored him, talking on his cell phone and complaining about not having the very same reports that P himself had presented to the group only moments before. Once excited to go to work, P says of that period, "The effort I put into my job dropped to about zero, and I felt totally devalued. From that point forward I put the minimal effort into my position." In fact, P was preparing to give notice when the company abruptly restructured and placed him under a new associate director.

Mercifully, his new boss was completely different—namely, calm, collected, and straightforward in her communication. P writes, "She is very consistent in what she wants. If I do something she doesn't want, she asks me to do it again, with specific direction." Because the communication is so clear and the manner respectful, P has begun to regain the passion he once had for his work and has also become more efficient in his follower role. He no longer wonders whether he is doing the right thing, or whether his boss will be satisfied, and so he no longer feels compelled to do extra work or take on extra projects.

This clarity has also relieved the anxiety around the value of his work, in general. He shares this insight: "Once I worked over the weekend to do a certain spreadsheet, but then on Monday she said it was the wrong one and a different one was needed. She wasn't upset and did not blame me at all. I realized in that moment that these changes are not personal. They just happen in the course of business. I accept that it's her job to make decisions and my job to do the work as best I can regardless of where it leads or doesn't lead."

This ability to let go of attachment in the followership role will come up again in chapter 6. For now, notice how the new leader's ability to be clear and neutral in her communication encourages strong performance and high engagement in the follower. P is able to enjoy his job again. The associate director often acknowledges the quality of his work and asks for his input on a regular basis.

Communication breakdowns produce heavy losses. In the first scenario, the director is not only unable or unwilling to articulate what he wants, but is also being disrespectful. P endures a stressful work environment, which lowers both the quality and quantity of his output and reduces his engagement level to zero. As he contemplates the prospect of searching for new employment, the company nearly loses a valuable and productive employee, one that will be difficult and costly to replace.

The second scenario demonstrates how quickly clear and considerate leadership can turn a situation like this around. In this case, the change came in the form of a completely new person, the associate director, who was capable of clear and precise thinking and communicating. But had the original director himself somehow been able to acquire these same skills, a similar transformation might have taken place, albeit with more difficulty.

The Follower's Role: Grant your full attention

Looks Like: Eye contact, focused body language, retention of spoken information, curiosity, nonjudgment, strategic deference

Benefit: Keeps you consistently well informed, accurate in understanding of needs and expectations, and able to relay details to others

Impact: Helps others to think and speak clearly

When It's Missing: Becoming easily distracted, interrupting, always speaking first, speaking for others, complaining, gossiping, criticizing, ignoring, spacing out, forgetting

The follower's view from the dance floor: *The song begins, and you stand to meet your partner. You lift your arms and create a flexible, relaxed shape to connect, consciously unlocking the joints in your wrists, elbows, and shoulders. You exhale and shift focus to your sense of touch, noting the multiple points of contact you have found along hands, arms, torso, back. Along these surfaces, you establish seamless, continuous, two-way communication, the conduit for your creative faculties to blend. You ground through the floor, shifting your weight forward, toward the balls of your feet. You narrow your balance even further, to the left foot only, between the first and second toes. You feel the strength of your entire left leg, the effort warming the muscles. Your right foot lightly skims the floor, sensing its texture. You note your partner's posture, tone, and energy. Your whole body listens.*

In this scene, the dancers are at the very beginning of their journey. The follower tunes in to the leader, focusing both on her own center of gravity and on the sensations of contact with the other person. If she does not do this, there is no way for the leader to communicate and begin the dance in the first place, much less navigate it successfully through to the end. In a work environment, we don't touch physically, but we can still tune in by observing body language, facial expression, and energy level in addition to words.

Granting someone your full attention is a powerful gift. Focusing on another person with curiosity and positive intent can uplift, center, and support that person; to give this kind of attention to someone is to affirm their intrinsic value and worthiness. By comparison, ignoring a person does the opposite; it diminishes their value. Giving supportive attention to colleagues and managers helps them remember and act from their own positive qualities, just as giving negative attention can elicit negative qualities. Granting someone your attention gives that person the empowering gift of being seen and heard, and the opportunity to share something of themselves— ideas, preferences, priorities, values—with you. It makes possible one of the primary acts of leadership: clear communication. As obvious as it may sound, only when employees are paying attention can managers successfully communicate ideas, instructions, needs, or objectives to them.

Receiving the attention of those in so-called *inferior* hierarchical positions is sometimes taken for granted by those in leadership positions, but it is nevertheless a choice that we make whenever we perform the role of the team member, or follower. Dancers in the leading role train to carefully solicit the following partner's attention, and check for it before communicating directional signals. They even pause mid-dance when they sense they have lost the follower's attention. Imagine what business meetings would be like if we applied this same guideline! Instead of taking it for granted, we might ask what would make employees *want* to grant their attention to their supervisor in the first place?

ACTIVE LISTENING

Active listening is the most direct way to give the gift of attention, and can be deceptively challenging. Ordinary listening is the kind that we tend to use for mundane transactions with restaurant staff and grocery cashiers. It's functional and, in many ways, scripted:

"Hello, how are you?"

"Fine, thank you!"

"What would you like?"

"I'll have a salad please."

The lines are familiar. We don't really need to listen because we already know what's coming.

Active listening is for conversations that have higher stakes, when we're exchanging insights or data that has far-reaching impact. In these cases, we don't know what's coming, and it's dangerous to think that we do. Relaxed and composed, active listening can provide a counterpoint to a team leader's energized state, and it can guide new thoughts into being. Unfortunately, we sometimes default into ordinary listening mode without realizing it, and then wonder why the conversation isn't productive.

When we're distracted by our own thoughts or by external events, our lack of attention can make others anxious or concerned about being heard or understood. These negative states alter the communication, making it rushed, loud, urgent, repetitive, or shorter or longer than necessary. When we force others to struggle for our attention, their energy is spent on that task, instead of on clearly communicating what we need to know.

By actively listening, we not only receive a thorough understanding of situations, needs, or challenges; we actually make it easier for our coworkers to think and speak to us calmly and clearly. By fully hearing what others are saying, we grasp both the big picture and the subtler details with more accuracy. And by consistently offering a receptive space for our colleagues and managers to express themselves verbally, they become more comfortable and skilled at doing so over time.

When you're not the one making decisions, it can be tempting to check out, to assume that because your role is not as visible, it is less important or even nonexistent. But there is great power in holding space for an idea to emerge or a decision to be made, and in responding to ideas and decisions with grace and commitment. By listening actively, we can actually draw out more inspired thoughts and ideas from our coworkers. Whether in the context of long-term project planning or short-term assignments, listening without agendas or assumptions is a crucial and learnable skill.

If you're unsure about the importance of listening, consider the concept of a sounding board, that person you call when you need to talk through an idea. You call a friend and spill out your thoughts for this person's receptive ear. Perhaps your friend's questions prompt you to clarify your priorities, or perhaps in simply expressing your thoughts aloud, a realization surfaces. Somehow your path forward becomes clearer, and your idea crystallizes into something articulate and actionable.

We do this naturally for one another in order to advance our thinking. Listening is an innate human skill, but it is also a professional skill, and it can be honed to a level at which conversations in meetings, on the phone, or around the table become more focused, creative, and insightful. Group discussions are an excellent example of how leading and following roles are naturally fluid. The person who is speaking, regardless of title, is playing the role of leader, and all others in the room, by default, are in the following role. Powerful speaking is a recognized and valued skill, but the ability to listen well is equally powerful.

YOUR INTERNAL STATE

A key to offering your attention as a gift is the habit of choosing your own internal state. It's easy to fall into negative patterns in stressful work environments, especially when learning something new, and many of us don't even realize we have a say in how we feel. In your own mind, do you tend to complain or to accept circumstances as they are? When things don't go the way you expect, do you tend to be critical or curious? Where in your work could you practice being more generous and encouraging, both toward yourself and toward others?

No matter what is happening outside of you, you can always choose what perspective to take, and you can always choose how to respond. Reclaiming this choice is essential for strong, impactful following. When you're out of your comfort zone in any way, do your best to be compassionate with yourself and use one of the following statements to reset your internal state:

Even though I'm feeling discomfort, I choose to stay open to learning.

Even though I'm feeling discomfort, I choose to be patient with myself and others.

Even though I'm feeling discomfort, I choose to experiment with new ways of communicating.

Even though I'm feeling discomfort, I choose to commit to my work.

Even though I'm feeling discomfort, I choose to believe everyone is doing the best they can.

Even though I'm feeling discomfort, I choose to _____.

OVERCOMING INTERNAL RESISTANCE

As a survival strategy, the brain naturally falls into repetitive patterns or familiar habits, both at work and in other areas of our lives. Familiar ways of working feel safe to us, but they don't usually feel very engaging. If we want to cultivate strong relationships, we need to venture into the unknown territory of change. But because even small changes can feel scary, our own minds tend to create resistance in order to make us feel safe again.

As you begin to experiment with the ways you play the following role, you will likely experience some amount of this resistance. Active, engaged following may be a whole new way of working for you, and it may influence many of your interpersonal interactions. You may encounter hidden assumptions and uncomfortable feeling states. You may notice yourself responding to others differently, or perhaps others will respond differently to you. Note that because their function is to keep us in familiar territory, resistance patterns can be tricky to identify. They can masquerade as fatigue, rationalization, procrastination, pessimism, defensiveness, or general negativity.

My client F is a self-employed graphic designer and works in a home office. He was feeling bored with his work and decided to enroll in an online art course to get some fresh ideas and boost his creativity. He was excited to get started, but when we checked in a couple of weeks later, he reluctantly admitted that he had been avoiding the new art assignments by cleaning the house. When I pressed, he complained, "The course is really repetitive. The instructor doesn't give clear instructions, and overall it's just not as structured as I was hoping." Notice how he's blaming the instructor, the leader in this relationship. To all of my questions about the course, F responded with criticism and disappointment. Once I saw this pattern, I asked if he might be simply encountering resistance.

Sure enough, underneath the cleaning and complaining, F was feeling lost and out of his comfort zone. Already a successful designer, he was terrified of failing at this new creative challenge, even though it was not tied directly to his professional work. Once he could articulate the feelings and accept they were normal, F was able to soften his critique of the art instructor and approach the course with lightness and a sense of adventure.

We are all human, and change is uncomfortable. There's a reason we resist: Growth makes us feel vulnerable, and because most of us have been culturally programmed to avoid it, vulnerability can make us defensive. Consider, instead, that our vulnerability might actually be an indication of our strength. It might be evidence that we are courageously learning and improving.

Do you feel tired, grouchy, angry, critical, distracted, argumentative, or avoidant at work? Here are some questions to ask yourself if you suspect that internal resistance is preventing you from giving your full attention to others. They may not remove your resistance altogether, but they may soften it just enough to get moving again.

Underneath my resistance, what am I fearing?

If I weren't feeling this resistance, what might I be open to learning?

If I weren't feeling this resistance, what might I be willing to try?

PRACTICING ATTENTION

Even if you think you're a good listener, the exercises below may strengthen your relationships with others and give more depth to your interactions. Try them out in advance of a group meeting or one-on-one conversation, or in situations where you know you have a tendency to become distracted.

Borrow a Memory: Before a conversation or meeting, choose a positive intention such as openness, acceptance, curiosity, calm, or receptivity, and recall a recent time in your life when you fully experienced this same state of being. Your memory need not include the people you work with or be related to work at all. For thirty seconds, time travel in your mind to this moment and feel what it was like to be there both physically and emotionally. Then come back to the present and keep your awareness on these sensations during the upcoming interaction.

Tune In: Notice the speaker's posture, expression, and energy level. Does the person seem tired, excited, relaxed, hurried, tentative, happy, worried, or something else? We naturally pick up on these tones nonverbally. Taking the time to acknowledge the whole person in front of you allows you to hear and understand them more fully, to contextualize their speech, and to choose a nonverbal attitude for yourself that can support them.

Be Still: Stand or sit in a relaxed state, unlock your joints, and allow your physical body to rest without moving.

Body/Breath/Mind: Bring your attention to your body and shift into a comfortable position. Then, bring your attention to your breath; often this will stimulate a deeper inhale. Without trying to change anything, observe your own inhale and exhale for three cycles. Finally, bring your attention to your mind and choose a deliberate orientation of receptivity to whatever the person in front of you is expressing.

Visual Focus: Look at the person who is speaking. This sounds simple, but it can feel uncomfortable if you are not used to it, or if you have a challenging history with the individual.

Take Turns: When someone else is speaking, wait until they are completely finished before responding. If you aren't sure, ask respectfully, "Are you finished?"

WHEN OTHERS ARE UNCLEAR

Focused attention can help others think and communicate more clearly. But relationships are a two-way street, and even if you give abundant attention and listen impeccably, others may still struggle to effectively communicate with you. After all, verbal and written communication are distinct skills themselves. It may seem that no matter how generously you give your attention or how closely you listen, you still don't understand what a manager or coworker wants. Resist the temptation to assign blame or slip into a negative internal state. It's tempting to get frustrated when others, especially those in formal leadership positions, aren't clear. As justified as you may feel in this, your frustration will not help either of you. Instead, try these techniques:

Assume Positive Intent: Remember that the other person is most likely not being vague on purpose. Assuming others are doing the best they can, no matter what, will turn your mind toward creative ways to address the situation.

Ask Clarifying Questions: It's important that your questions are direct and specific, so that the other person can focus on relevant details. Consider the following examples:

"What do you need from me on Monday?"

"Could you tell me who to speak with about x?"

"Can you describe what you see happening in the next stage of the project?"

"What does done look like?"

Orientation: You can give the other person an anchor by focusing on a project or area of concern that they have already expressed and then asking for more detail. Consider the following examples:

"You mentioned project A. Can you say more about what you'd like done on that this week?"

"You mentioned client account B. Can you tell me more about our next steps with them?"

CHAPTER 2:
INCLUSION AND ENGAGEMENT

INCLUSION
+
ENGAGEMENT

The Leader's Role: Facilitate participation

Looks Like: Welcoming input, ensuring everyone has the opportunity to speak, offering multiple avenues of participation, opening meetings with creative icebreakers, meeting with team members individually, implementing race and gender equity practices, expressing gratitude and appreciation in specific terms

Benefit: Gathers a wide variety of viewpoints; establishes shared purpose, belonging, and commitment

Impact: Encourages others to share data, insights, ideas, concerns, and perspectives

When It's Missing: Favoring certain members of the group while ignoring others, discrimination, nepotism, monologues, aggressive speech or behavior, avoiding interaction

---

In a dance for two, there's no denying the need for the other person. Inclusion is built in. For leaders in particular, an elaborate ritual of eye contact and silent gesture emphasizes the importance of inviting a single, specific follower to dance. Further, social dancers don't just partner with one person. They might dance with a dozen different people in a single evening, and the next night, a dozen more. Beyond acknowledgment of the pair dynamic, there is a high value placed on the community-building aspect of social dance, on meeting new people in new places, and on welcoming beginners. Dancers understand that we need each other in order to thrive, and that success is always a shared phenomenon.

Imagine taking this perspective into work with you, looking around at your coworkers, and thinking to yourself, *I need these people in order to do my job. I depend on them. They make what I do possible. I have this job because of them.* You may not think about your career with the same excitement that social dancers bring to their dancing. Still, the analogy is an interesting one because it fundamentally changes how we see our colleagues and how we value our relationships with them.

In *The Power of Followership*, one of the earliest works on the subject, Robert E. Kelley observes that followers—or at least followership activities—are responsible for over 80 percent of any group's success. He writes,

> Without followers, little gets done; with them, mountains get moved. By sheer numbers alone, followers represent the bulk and substance of any enterprise. Fundamentally, we must begin to see that the errors of leadership are better overcome and the triumphs of history are better achieved by engaging everyone's heroism rather than waiting for some improbable hero to emerge.[13]

This perspective offers an important alternative to the hidden bias of *mirrortocracy* and the narrative of the *high-potential* employee.

---

13   Kelley, *The Power of Followership*, 21.

A truly inclusive approach to leadership focuses on cultivating high potential generally, not only in certain individuals.

L took a position as executive director of a small arts nonprofit, and carefully recruited a board of directors who would support the organization's original vision. Despite his best efforts, however, some members of the community began to complain about the organization's programs, claiming they were a waste of time and didn't address their priorities. He reflects many years later, "I was naïve, I think, in assuming that everyone would want to support these programs. Lots of people were enthusiastic about them, but not everyone. I don't think I really understood what was most important to certain segments of the community." After a series of new conversations with a wider range of community members, L and the board of directors shifted their plans for the following year. Some programs disappeared, but others became more stable. Because L found a way to include more voices, the organization became stronger and more aligned with the community it was founded to represent.

There are many ways to encourage and value others, the most important of which is expressing a sincere desire to hear what they have to say. Had L cast a wider net at the beginning, he may have gained more momentum and support early on. Rather than restructuring, he might have spent those first few years investing in programs that would have the long-term support of the community. He was able to recover, but the early missteps permanently soured his relationship with certain segments of the community.

The Follower's Role: Help develop ideas
Looks Like: Asking thoughtful questions, providing relevant information, proposing alternative scenarios, preparing in advance
Benefit: Demonstrates your value to the team or to supervisors, allows greater influence on projects and decision-making
Impact: Allows others to see from different perspectives
When It's Missing: Giving unsolicited advice; making inappropriate, redundant, or uninformed comments; checking out in meetings; failing to prepare

The follower's view from the dance floor: *As you feel the pressure change along your arm and left side of your torso, your right leg reaches out to take the first step. Gliding along the floor, your movement mirrors the leader's signal. You take several steps together at the same, even rhythm, then pause. Your left leg is free now—you tap it gently against the floor, marking the percussion line in the song. As you do this, you slightly squeeze both hands to let the leader know you are adding this small flourish, a subtle decoration of the sequence she has just composed for the two of you. You return to your neutral hold at the end of the phrase, just as she sends the next signal. Your ideas overlap by mere flashes of time, flowing together like instruments blending in an orchestra.*

In this scene, the dancers take their first steps together. In general, directions flow from leader to follower as a couple makes their way around the floor, but in musical interpretation, the dialogue between partners becomes more nuanced, with skilled followers inserting tiny flourishes, accents, and pauses, often at transition points between phrases. They might also slightly slow down or speed up certain movements in response to the musical dynamics in a particular arrangement. In this way, followers elevate the artistry of the dance by making subtle, mindful contributions, illustrating the complementary nature of the two roles.

Rather than a stereotypical silence or compliance, the dancer's notion of following is more accurately practiced at work by speaking up, with sensitivity to the context, to help develop ideas and inform decisions. A counterpoint to the leading skill of facilitating inclusive meetings or discussions, skillful following might take the form of a single, well-placed question or observation. When communication is tactfully offered from the following side of a conversation, it serves the interests of the group, helping to clarify, correct, and fine-tune proposals, projects, and timelines.

MINDFUL PARTICIPATION

During in-person gatherings and informal conversations, participation is usually verbal, requiring both the wisdom and the confidence to find, or sometimes create, a moment to speak. Contributions need not be earth-shattering nor revolutionary in nature. In fact, often simple, concise questions and observations are the ones that turn thinking around and reveal hidden gems. Staying curious and thinking critically as you talk with others may result in plans that are far better than any one person could have come up with alone. In this context, the art of following is in the timing and relevance of the content, much like a dancer adding a subtle twist or flourish at the end of a sequence, or delaying just a slight amount so that a movement synchronizes exactly with the musical phrase. Subtle, but powerful.

Interrupting the flow of the conversation or derailing a meeting on an unrelated tangent are not examples of effective, mindful participation. When we restate others' ideas, overexplain, or attempt to dominate the conversation, we are not supporting the team or moving the work forward. However, the narrow, on-the-ground viewpoint of the following role does give individual employees the ability to point out important details that supervisors might not have considered, especially about the practical, real-world implications of higher-level decisions. Those working in supporting roles may know the best tool for the job, or how much time a task will take to complete and the risks it entails. Providing this information in a timely and appropriate fashion is essential, as it can prevent potential problems and save both time and resources. But it may not always feel natural, especially if you are new in your role or if the group you're a part of has an established rhythm of its own.

S led a research team of seven other scientists in a startup biotechnology company, and she herself reported to two separate vice presidents. At regular weekly meetings, the VPs would frequently become distracted and forget to address her agenda items. She recalls, "Sometimes new agenda items would appear that I wasn't aware of, and the whole time would be spent on those. My points were not addressed in a way that was actionable, or they were just dismissed altogether. It was really annoying. I kept thinking, *Why am I here? Can I just go back to my lab?*"

In our coaching, S and I worked on shifting her mindset around participation, and after a few weeks, she did begin to speak up, politely requesting the conversation include her questions. She had to step out of her comfort zone to do this, especially because her superiors did not immediately respond any differently. She had to repeat herself several times, and recalls a significant stylistic difference in their modes of communication. "It felt like arguing to me, but to them I think it just felt like discussion."

After several attempts, however, she was able to express herself in concise statements that explained the potential negative consequences of overlooking her team's concerns. She describes the shift this way: "I started thinking of this as a dance where you don't just stop—you keep moving with them and stay engaged. It's a choice to keep trying to find more intentional ways of communicating."

A combination of persistence and specific language got the VPs' attention, and those meetings became more productive. Her team was able to move ahead with projects that were previously stalled.

Generally, we serve our teams best when we share information in ways that do not excessively disrupt or distract from the flow of business. Otherwise, our contributions may be overlooked, dismissed, or rejected. In special cases, however, disruption may be called for. S walked a fine line between interrupting the meeting and advocating for very real business concerns that the VPs were simply not aware of, or perhaps not taking seriously enough.

We all have ways of interacting with others that we find more comfortable, and often those default tendencies vary depending on whether the interaction is in person or remote, whether you are speaking one-on-one or in a group, or whether the context is formal or informal. Speaking frequently does not necessarily mean that your participation is useful or relevant. Likewise, silence does not necessarily indicate disengagement or lack of influence. Sometimes knowing what *not* to say is as crucial as knowing what *to* say.

In addition to live conversation, we participate in writing through email and on digital platforms. Written communication need not be frequent or elaborate to be effective. A concise, specific comment is likely more helpful than several paragraphs that restate known information. Sometimes, it may be most helpful to deliberately *not* participate, to be selective in whom we communicate with, or to simply wait until later. Before offering an idea, question, or piece of information, try asking yourself, *How can I best support this process?*. Becoming more mindful in your participation begins by recognizing your own default patterns, and then asking yourself some honest questions to evaluate what adjustments might make your contributions more valuable. Some of these changes may take you out of your comfort zone. Ask for feedback to get a sense of how your actions are being perceived.

TALK TO THINK OR THINK TO TALK

There is no one way to communicate effectively, and we each have a natural bias in how we express ourselves. At the same time, being aware of that bias and challenging it can be a growth opportunity. Do you tend to formulate an idea in your own mind, and then share it aloud? Or do you, rather, formulate ideas in real time as you speak? Take a moment to consider at which end of the spectrum you fall.

If you tend to be more outgoing socially, you may likely talk to think, speaking easily and frequently whether in groups or in private conversations. If this is your natural pattern, you may want to practice holding back and listening to what others are saying first, before adding your own thoughts. The temptation for those who process thoughts aloud is to value interaction over ideas. Curbing this impulse can save time and boost your credibility by ensuring that what you contribute is concise, clear, and distinct from what has already been expressed.

If you find yourself on the other end of the spectrum, thinking before speaking, you may want to consider preparing your own notes in advance so that you can join the discussion a little sooner. The risk for those who process thoughts silently is that they may keep an idea to themselves until a decision has already been made. One mind working on a problem is rarely as strong as several. By sharing your ideas, the group benefits from an additional perspective, and your own thinking becomes sharper and more flexible.

PROVING OR SOLVING

When we work in high-pressure environments, it can be tempting to orient our thinking and therefore our communication toward proving our worth and value rather than toward solving a real problem. This may seem like hair-splitting, because solving problems in many ways *does* prove your value, but there is an important difference. When you are focused on the work itself, and on your part in a collective effort, the ways in which you show up and participate are more likely to lean toward pragmatic problem-solving. By comparison, when you worry about how others may be evaluating you or your performance, it's more likely that you'll come across as self-centered or confrontational as you try to prove your worth.

Communication that *proves* is appropriate in certain contexts, but not usually in the everyday rhythm of working together. Common examples include informing others of your accomplishments, expressing general knowledge, offering unsolicited advice or opinions, and responding to specific requests with unrelated or tangential information. Underneath these proving patterns, there might be a fear of not knowing something, or an underlying assumption that you should already know everything related to your job. If you resonate with this sentiment, pay attention to it, because it likely influences the ways in which you communicate with others, especially with those holding formal leadership titles. Even thinking proving thoughts in the privacy of your own mind can adversely impact your words and nonverbal signals.

In contrast, *solving* patterns tend to feature questions and neutral observations. An attitude of solving connects the dots between data points, allowing past experience to inform current thinking. Holding the intention of curiosity is an effective way to get familiar with the *solving* way of thinking and speaking. Consider the following questions:

What's something I've said to a colleague recently when I was feeling the need to prove my own competence?

How might I have responded differently if I had chosen to simply be curious about the subject or the outcome?

PRACTICING ENGAGEMENT

Even if you are comfortable talking with others, the exercises below may strengthen your ability to add value with what you say or don't say. Try them out in your next group meeting or one-on-one conversation, especially in situations where you know you have a tendency to either talk too much or hold back your ideas.

Prepare: The more familiar you are with the subject or situation being discussed, the more likely you'll be able to offer a novel perspective or relevant details about it.

Data Point: Ask yourself, *What's the one piece of information I have that could make a difference in this conversation?* You don't need to make a proposal—it's often enough to just offer the information that you feel is relevant and that hasn't yet been spoken aloud.

Open-Ended Questions: When you feel an idea isn't fully formed, or that you don't understand it completely, asking for more detail in an open-ended way can be informative for the entire group. Your question invites deeper exploration around the idea itself, like the following examples:

"Could you speak more about *x* idea?"

"Could you share a little more about how this idea developed?"

What If: This is one way to get yourself thinking creatively about any subject. Imagine a variety of scenarios relevant to the work. It may help to put yourself in the client or customer's shoes. You can express the what-if statements to the group verbally, or use this as a personal preparation strategy to generate new ideas before an upcoming meeting.

"What if we had a feature that could do *x*?"

"What if the customer has *y* problem?"

"What if there could be a faster way to get *z* done?"

Backup: If someone else shares an idea you resonate strongly with, add your support verbally, but concisely, without restating anything. If appropriate, provide additional data or rationale to support the idea:

"I agree with Maria's point."

"I agree with Maria's point, and [data] and [rationale] also suggest the same conclusion."

Say It Once: Some of us have the tendency to repeat ourselves when expressing a thought, or restate the same thing in different ways multiple times. Before you speak, take a moment to formulate your thought in your mind, then just say it once and let it stand.

Be Kind: No matter what you plan to say, saying it with kindness can increase the chances that it will be well received. Check your own irritation or impatience, and speak with an intention of generosity.

WHEN OTHERS LEAVE YOU OUT

When others don't seem open to dialogue, especially managers and supervisors, it can seem challenging (or even impossible) to engage with them. The other person may feel pressured for time, may have a blind spot, or may not feel comfortable with or experienced in the role she is in. Depending on the situation, these techniques may help you communicate even when others don't seem accessible.

Reroute Communication: If it's not possible to communicate with a manager or point person directly, but you're holding on to important information or need something urgently, communicate with other team members instead. The information may reach the one who needs to hear it through another channel, or you may discover another way to get what you need.

Change Modes: If verbal communication isn't working, try writing instead. If email isn't producing a response, try a handwritten note or a phone call.

Acknowledge: Thank your manager or colleague, or acknowledge the value of his or her work, time, and/or attention. When the other person appears to be inconsiderate, it may indicate a need to feel valued. If you can sincerely provide this, it may strengthen the rapport between you. Consider the following examples:

"I want to thank you for getting me that information yesterday. I really appreciate it."

"I realize your time is valuable, and I really appreciate you making time for this meeting."

"The work you finished last week made a huge difference for me. I was able to get the next piece of design work done for [team project or deadline]."

Label:[14] Use phrases that begin with *It seems like* or *It sounds like* to name stressors, fears, or concerns from the other person's point of view, no matter how irrational or ridiculous. Do your best to imagine what the other person may be feeling, even if you disagree with their opinion or feel they are wrong. Put your own feelings aside. Consider the following examples:

"It seems like things are really stressful for you right now."

"It sounds like you're under a lot of pressure this week."

"It looks like I'm not the first person to ask you for something this morning."

---

14   Inspired by the concept of *tactical empathy*, a technique described by Chris Voss in *Never Split the Difference.*

CHAPTER 3:
CARE AND OPENNESS

CARE
+
OPENNESS

The Leader's Role: Keep others safe

Looks Like: Projecting kindness, acceptance and nonjudgment; hearing concerns; aligning feedback with stated goals; mediating disagreements fairly; acknowledging stress and anxiety; arranging celebrations of achievements; requesting feedback

Benefit: Facilitates a healthy flow of information and ideas within a team or group, develops loyalty and trust

Impact: Encourages others to grow professionally and personally

When It's Missing: Excessive competitiveness, taking others for granted, ignoring concerns and problems, taboo subjects, dismissing feelings, pejorative language, screaming

---

A crowded dance floor demands that leaders learn to practice the equivalent of driver safety. They must be able to navigate available space without crashing into other couples or putting their partners at risk of being stepping on, kicked, or scratched by another dancer's fast-moving stiletto heel. Followers on the dance floor walk backward—they literally can't see where they are going. And because social dancers improvise, followers train to focus on the present moment, one step at a time. Only the leader sees a few precious moments into the future, and steers accordingly. This perceptual advantage comes with the responsibility to physically protect one's partner. Leaders who develop a track record of safe and skillful navigation are highly regarded in the community and serve as role models for beginners.

Physical safety is, indeed, a primary concern in many lines of work; just think of industries such as healthcare, construction, manufacturing, or energy. But even when we do not face physical danger in our work, caring leaders earn respect and loyalty in much the same way—by providing cover when their team members take professional risks, supporting them in speaking candidly, and looking out for their career interests over time.

B was director of data analytics for his department. When a new department supervisor was hired, he was already thinking of leaving the company because he no longer felt challenged or engaged in his work. Fortunately, the new supervisor deliberately built a strong rapport with B, asked him to share his perspective on how the department was currently running, and generally made herself available as a professional resource.

Because the supervisor intentionally established a sense of safety up front, B soon felt comfortable approaching her about his desire to pursue opportunities not available in his current position. As a result of their candid dialogue, she was able to help him transfer laterally to a different section of the company where he could develop his career in a more fulfilling role. That supervisor prevented the loss of a valuable employee by establishing a safe environment to talk about issues that matter, and B provided strong support for the on-boarding of his replacement.

Professional caring is often about establishing this kind of psychological safety. We need to know it's okay to be who we are and feel what we feel. Emotions are still taboo in most work environments, tacking right alongside the ideas of following and femininity, but a growing body of research makes the case that excluding this aspect of our nature is detrimental, even dangerous. In *Emotional Intelligence*, psychologist Daniel Goleman writes,

> There is growing evidence that fundamental ethical stances in life stem from underlying emotional capacities. For one, impulse is the medium of emotion; the seed of all impulse is a feeling bursting to express itself in action. Those who are at the mercy of impulse—who lack self-control—suffer a moral deficiency. The ability to control impulse is the base of will and character. By the same token, the root of altruism lies in empathy, the ability to read emotions in others; lacking a sense of another's need or despair, there is no caring. And if there are any two moral stances that our times call for, they are precisely these, self-restraint and compassion.[15]

Emotional intelligence has been linked with mindfulness. In order to prevent anxieties of various kinds from taking over our higher-level thinking, we need to be aware that those feelings are present in the first place and have strategies to shift into calmer states by adjusting our focus. Likewise, it's crucial to notice when others are distressed and to interact with them appropriately. Those in leadership roles are positioned to value, encourage, and facilitate the cultivation of emotional intelligence in their teams and organizations. Unfortunately, this kind of supportive connection between leader and follower doesn't exist in every workplace.

J worked for many years as a physician in emergency rooms, and watched nurses and other doctors often ignore, mistreat, or misdiagnose patients who were suffering, some of them small

---

15   Goleman, *Emotional Intelligence*, xii.

children and babies. I asked her about the concept of emotional safety in her environment, and whether she felt the lack of this had played a role in the behavior of the medical staff. She writes, "Tragically, distancing yourself from patients and shutting down emotionally is completely normalized in medical environments. You're already exhausted. The last thing you need to do for your own health is to muffle or suppress your emotions. Emotional responses impact our decisions, whether we're aware of them or not. Being aware of your own emotional state completely changes the kind of care that you give. The consequences of emotional shutdown can be a cruel and inhumane treatment of patients, which borders on unethical."

Certainly, we need medical professionals to develop a certain tolerance around human distress, injury, and disease, but when healthcare professionals do not believe it is okay for them to express natural empathic responses, something is wrong. Normalizing human feeling not only serves the well-being of healthcare staff members themselves, but also ensures quality humane care for all of the patients those staff members serve.

Our emotions are, in fact, a huge part of what makes us intelligent. We don't necessarily want them running the show, but we need them as a kind of internal board of advisors. When we block our feelings, we can no longer respond appropriately to the people around us. Blocked emotional material, over time, builds a distorted perception of the world that masquerades as rational understanding. False premises produce false logic. As J describes, our own perceptions and judgment calls can be distorted by tuning out our emotions and reducing our capacity for empathy.

In dance, the leader uses a vertical body posture to establish a consistent point of reference for followers, in spatial terms. Follower partners orient their movement around the leader's centerline, as a craftsman might draw a perfect circle around the point of a compass. The couple's circle is the safe zone for movement, where the follower can freely express the shape, style, and personality of the dance through spiraling, arcing, extending, and condensing movements. At work, leaders can establish a comparable *emotional* safe zone for followers around themselves and throughout their work environments by practicing acceptance and nonjudgment, treating team members with fairness and consideration, and acting to facilitate their success.

This does not mean the leader becomes a de facto therapist or the recipient of endless complaints. Rather, the emotional safe zone helps others let their feelings flow through and exit the nervous system so that they can think more clearly and get their work done. This is especially true in the context of professional disagreement, conflict, or other work-related stress. When you see your team members struggling, holding a steady internal reference point can be a huge help.

The Follower's Role: Choose trust

Looks Like: Receiving and implementing constructive feedback, speaking tactfully in moments of disagreement without becoming defensive

Benefit: Provides practical insights for growth and advancement, strengthens relationships, demonstrates reliability

Impact: Encourages others to speak honestly and authentically

When It's Missing: Becoming defensive or angry, making excuses, ignoring feedback or suggestions, arguing, insulting or putting others down, sabotaging projects, undermining team goals

---

The follower's view from the dance floor: *You can't see behind you, but you reach your leg back anyway, smoothly and without hesitation. You feel only air above your calf—the breeze from a fan somewhere in the corner. You close your eyes and shift focus to the sensation of your thin-soled shoe sliding against the hardwood, toes pressing down for stability, and of the stretch through your waist as you twist left, then right, then left again. Your leader tenses and halts, and you pull back in a reflex reaction, contracting your shoulder blades and bracing your arms stiffly. The moment passes, and you relax everything again, softening your grip and shifting your weight slightly forward. Soon, you move again, and your steps begin to flow once more. You sink into the rhythm, your walk marking the tempo of the song.*

In this scene, the follower deliberately relaxes into her partner's embrace again after a momentary break. She trusts the leader to navigate the dance floor, which she cannot see, one step at a time. Improvising, she does not know what is coming next, but continues to follow the leader anyway. This choice keeps her anchored in the present moment and able to instantly reconnect. Indeed, it permits the dance to continue.

Openness can feel like something we either have or don't have, like an automatic on-off switch that's out of our control. We're open or we're closed. We might associate openness and trust only with our friends and family, or perhaps with colleagues that we get along with easily. With everyone else, though, we just don't have it. It may be tempting to assume you can't be open with others, especially managers and supervisors, unless they first prove themselves worthy. Dancers, however, regularly practice openness with total strangers. It is part of their basic tool kit, and one of reasons that social dance is such a powerful force of community-building. Rather than on or off, their understanding of openness is more like a dimmer that they continually adjust. And just as a colleague or manager who creates a safe environment is easier to trust, choosing to be open with others in the first place encourages them to be trust*worthy.*

CHOOSING TRUST

Choosing to trust others, especially in moments of uncertainty, is a courageous act. It orients us in body and mind toward generosity, goodwill, and possibility. In his book *The Trust Factor*, neuroeconomist Paul Zak writes, "Trust profoundly improves organizational performance by providing the foundation for effective teamwork and intrinsic motivation."[16] Without trust, every request, suggestion, and comment from another person becomes a suspicious one, subject to evaluation and scrutiny. Without trust, we feel unsafe, and so we guard against imagined threats and unintended offenses. A lack of openness eventually becomes defensiveness.

Although perhaps counterintuitive, it's worth challenging the assumption that others need to earn our trust. We're used to holding trust out like a prize to be bestowed only when it's fully and undeniably deserved. It's important to hold others accountable for their actions, but withholding trust purely out of caution, rather than because of any known reason, can prevent us from developing healthy, balanced relationships. It can put us into an endless loop in our own minds. How do we know we can trust another person? How much proof is enough?

When those in leadership positions factor everyone else's professional interests into their decisions, it is obviously much easier to trust them, but the active choice to trust in the first place can help solicit that same kind of consideration. That consideration may include ensuring our physical safety, as it does in dance, but it also means looking out for our professional well-being in general. What do we need in order to best do our work? Managers and supervisors who seek to provide these things, whether they be extra notebooks, security cameras, or budget-line items, inspire trust and loyalty. We can encourage this kind of behavior, which I refer to as *care* at the beginning of this chapter, by deliberately choosing to trust coworkers and leaders, even before they have earned it.

---

16   Zak, *The Trust Factor*, 7.

Choosing an attitude of trust over suspicion can have a striking effect on outward professional communication, both verbal and nonverbal. When we choose openness, the body relaxes, standing and speaking with less effort. We can listen better and fully take in what others are saying. We have a natural desire to help one another because we feel, on a visceral level, that we are on the same team. When we stay open to a range of perspectives and feedback, we lose some of our fear of judgment and become more confident about who we are and what we do.

S is a physical therapist (PT) at a busy outpatient clinic. She writes, "There are many professional disagreements between PTs at work. We all have a different focus, and different tools and ideas when it comes to treating a patient. In my team of seven outpatient PTs, we have built a community of open sharing, asking questions, friendly disagreements. The general rules that keep this community strong are holding a safe space for open communication, checking ego at the door, being humble, and having compassion. We work hard, and we take excellent care of our patients." Since every therapist works independently within the same clinic, there is no single leader, per se, in this group. Still, the practice of openness strengthens all of its members. S goes on to describe what happens when this trait is missing: "Other teams at the hospital do not have this kind of bond, and they have high staff tension, poor communication, safety concerns, and patient-care errors."

When our coworkers and team leaders feel that we trust them, they are more likely to encourage us to stretch our own professional limits, and to back us up when we take creative risks. When others sense mistrust and suspicion, however, they act more conservatively and with more control, narrowing the scope of our work or making it more difficult for us to engage and grow.

Performance reviews and one-on-ones are crucial opportunities to actively choose openness. In any situation in which we are receiving feedback on our work, openness is not only in our own best interest but also in everyone's. To stay open, we must choose to believe that the other person wants to lift us up, not cut us down. We have to remember that the purpose of feedback is not to criticize or belittle us, but to support our growth. One way to do this is to focus on the information itself, regardless of the tone or style of its delivery. If we can intentionally stay open rather than get defensive, we stand to gain valuable insights that will help us in our own careers and allow us to make more valuable contributions. Others will speak more candidly and authentically when they know we are open to what they have to share.

Trusting on purpose can feel vulnerable, especially when you don't know your coworkers very well. Admittedly, it's a leap of faith, but one that is better taken than shied away from. We should never blindly trust others regardless of their actions, but even in the absence of any evidence, many of us default toward suspicion, and then struggle to connect with others. By giving your colleagues the benefit of the doubt, you can establish healthy relationships faster and lay a foundation for clear communication and mutual support.

Note: In work environments where leaders have repeatedly violated our trust, this approach may not be appropriate. Instead, we might request and in some cases insist that leaders demonstrate specific acts of protection and care before considering whether to give them our trust again.

RECEIVING FEEDBACK

Although most of us receive feedback on a regular basis, it can still be a challenge for our minds to distinguish between criticism of our *work* and criticism of the *self*. This is why many of us dread feedback, or feel the need to "steel ourselves" before walking into a review meeting. It's one of the places where we're at risk of becoming defensive, and where we therefore benefit greatly from practicing openness. It's what helps us stay accountable to others and committed to our own career goals.

One of my clients, now retired from a supervisory position, described how the process impacted her relationships with direct reports: "Many of my junior team members didn't realize that how they took feedback changed how I saw them and what happened next. If they were able to take the feedback well, the relationship deepened, especially if they could perceive that my comments were intended for their growth. But those who resisted usually missed out on future opportunities."

Though we may not realize it in the moment, resistance to feedback erodes connection. It suggests to leaders that we aren't willing or able to learn, or that we simply aren't ready for more complex work yet. By welcoming feedback and acting on it immediately, we invite stronger assignments and inspire leaders to take risks with us and to provide more opportunities to build skills and knowledge.

Defensiveness is a common survival reflex, usually triggered by old patterns of insecurity, but it's counterproductive in contemporary work environments. If you are feeling angry or agitated, making excuses, or arguing, you may have accidentally slipped into defensiveness. It's normal, and we all trip that wire from time to time. The antidote is to flip the accountability switch as soon as possible, because we can't be defensive and accountable at the same time.

You know you've switched when you're taking a genuine interest in the feedback you're receiving, and when you realize that it's a useful way to improve your own work and grow in your career. Being able to receive feedback gracefully is also about understanding that your work matters because it directly impacts other people. Mistakes happen. If you're in defensive mode, you'll tend to ignore and likely repeat them. If you commit to staying open and accountable, on the other hand, you can own your mistakes and correct them in the future. Here's how:

Frame: Determine what your own broad, professional goals are so that you can look for ways that the feedback might support you in reaching them. No matter what the feedback is or how it is given, there is always a way to find value in the exchange.

Sphere of Work: Visualize a large sphere that represents your entire self, and then place another, smaller sphere inside it, to represent your work. Choose different colors for the large and small spheres. Mentally "sit" in the larger sphere of yourself, and look objectively at your work sphere to assess how the feedback can best support its growth and well-being.

Depersonalize: The idea of depersonalizing direct feedback may sound illogical because, of course, the feedback is being given to *you*, and is based on *your* work. However, the feedback is also, always, about the person giving it. Both the content and the delivery of the feedback is as much a reflection of the speaker's background, expertise, priorities, and attitude as it is about you or your work. That is why different people often offer different feedback, or might say the same thing in very different ways. Depersonalizing does not mean that you disregard the feedback. Rather, it is a way for you to understand it more accurately. Ask yourself the following:

What's important to this person, that they are giving me this feedback?

If I were sitting on their side of the table, what might concern me the most about my work and why?

Get Specific: The more clearly you understand the feedback, the better able you will be to determine how, or if, you will be able to act on it. Asking clarifying questions about the specific events or tasks in question also demonstrates to the speaker that you are listening, that you value the feedback, and that you are committed to your own growth.

Take Action: Even if you feel terrible about the feedback, choose at least one thing to do immediately that will help you learn something new or strengthen an existing skill. Move the thinking mind out of the way, and get something done that is relevant to the feedback. The act of doing persuades your nervous system that you are safe and that it is okay to relax, and your behavior also sends a message to others that you are committed to improvement. If you're not sure what to do, ask yourself, *How I can use this feedback to further my own goals or support my own general well-being?*

SELF-ASSESSMENT ON RECEIVING FEEDBACK

Consider a few recent situations in which you received feedback from a colleague or supervisor. Do you always respond to feedback in the same way? Or does your internal state depend on the context, the person, or some other variable? Consider the two positions in the chart below, *disempowered* and *empowered*, and then answer the self-inquiry questions to start learning how to recognize each one within yourself.

Disempowered Position	Empowered Position
Seeing feedback as an opportunity to judge or be judged	Seeing feedback as an opportunity to grow or facilitate growth
Responding with defensiveness	Responding with accountability

How do I typically respond to feedback?

How do I feel, think, and speak when I put myself in a position of defensiveness?

How do I feel, think, and speak when I put myself in a position of accountability?

What's one thing I can do to remind myself to act from accountability?

NAVIGATING DISAGREEMENT

Arguments are never fun, but more importantly, they are usually a considerable waste of time and energy. Different from productive disagreement, which can actually be a creative process in itself, an argument occurs when we stop listening to one another and simply defend opposing positions. What keeps us stuck in an argument with another person is usually the same thing that keeps us stuck in our own minds: black-and-white thinking, just like the on-off openness switch. In disagreement, the solution is usually waiting for us in the gray area, and we slowly find our way to it by hearing one another's differing perspectives on the same situation, and by considering many possible approaches.

But if we allow disagreement to escalate into a full-blown argument, we lose the creative opportunity to discover a new shade of gray. Here are some suggestions for staying open in moments of disagreement:

Silence: Resist the urge to fight. Instead, listen to the words your colleague is actually saying. Anything that directly contradicts these words in the moment is likely to be perceived as an attack and could provoke a fight/flight/freeze response, the hallmark of a nonproductive argument. Offense is balanced by defense. The less you oppose or attack the idea in question, the less likely you'll trigger a defense of that idea. *Note: If silence feels like shutting down for you, use one of the other techniques in this section.*

Exhale: Note what you are feeling and where you are feeling it in your own body. Exhale fully into this area. By intentionally focusing on the exhale, you stimulate the parasympathetic nervous system, the switch that signals relaxation. Because humans tend to mirror one another, doing this offers a silent invitation for others to relax as well.

Get Curious: Ask questions that solicit the other person's point of view. It is not important whether you agree with the point of view—only that your colleague is able to fully express it. Being heard is one of our most primary needs. By meeting this need, you can help others shift out of fight/flight/freeze mode and into a more relaxed state where productive disagreement can occur.

Acknowledgment: Thank the other person for expressing his or her view. If possible, end the conversation with an agreement to continue later when you've both had some time to reflect.

Neutral Tone: If a decision is necessary soon, ask permission to express your own perspective. Express your view in a neutral tone, without critiquing or discounting the other person's view. In your mind, allow both perspectives to exist simultaneously without the need for one to win. Trust that a resolution can be found, even if you can't see it yet.

SELF-ASSESSMENT ON NAVIGATING DISAGREEMENT

Consider a few recent situations in which you experienced disagreement with a colleague or supervisor. Do you always respond to disagreement in the same way? Or does your internal state depend on the context, the person, or some other variable? Consider the two positions in the chart below, *disempowered* and *empowered*, and then answer the self-inquiry questions to start learning how to recognize each one within yourself.

Disempowered Position	Empowered Position
Seeing disagreement as an opportunity to win or lose	Seeing disagreement as an opportunity to co-create
Responding with judgment	Responding with curiosity

How do I typically behave when I disagree with others?
How do I feel, think, and speak when I put myself in a position of judgment?

How do I feel, think, and speak when I put myself in a position of curiosity?

What's one thing I can do to remind myself to choose curiosity?

PRACTICING OPENNESS

Cultivating openness as a skill requires us to mentally press the pause button on our automatic defense mechanisms, and to deliberately look for evidence of safety instead. This can feel a little artificial, even counterintuitive, but it gets easier with practice. Try these techniques proactively, outside of more highly charged situations like receiving feedback or experiencing disagreement.

Take a Break: Taking breaks periodically throughout the day can increase levels of physical and emotional comfort and well-being. Eat lunch away from your desk, take a quick walk, or focus on something you're grateful for.

Relax the Body: Our protective habits are most noticeable in our muscles and in our posture. If you are experiencing tension or constriction, chances are that you are unconsciously protecting yourself from a potential threat, whether real or imagined. Relaxing the body is a direct way to interrupt these survival reflexes and retrain ourselves to feel safe at work.

Internal Narrative: Most of us have running commentaries about every person we meet and every situation we are in. If you notice your own thoughts throughout the day, you may be surprised by them! When we have difficulty staying open, there is likely a very specific assumption we are making about a certain person or about people in general. For example, *People always stab you in the back*, or *My manager is on a power trip*. Take charge of these narratives and give them a thorough edit. When you start telling yourself a more neutral, optimistic, or compassionate story, you may find it easier to trust others.

Small Talk: I define *small talk* as friendly verbal conversation that builds rapport and is based on exchanging small bits of personal information. Demonstrating interest in another person for who they are—not for what they do—establishes and reinforces familiarity. And familiarity encourages our nervous system to relax and trust those around us, laying the foundation for more complex conversation later. Here's an example:

Alex: "What did you do over the weekend?"

Brian: "I went for a hike Sunday morning with some friends. How about you?"

Alex: "I tried out a new bread recipe—I really like to bake, and I only have time to do it on the weekends."

Brian: "Mmm, fresh bread. Any leftovers?"

Alex: "Not this time, but I'll keep you in mind! Where did you go hiking?"

Sharing these simple experiences makes the two people in this example feel that they know one another a bit more than they did a few moments ago, and that sense of knowing sends messages of trust and safety through the nervous system. When these same two people meet next week to discuss a business proposal, they'll still have the physical memory of feeling safe around one another, which increases the chances of their business meeting being authentic and collaborative.

WHEN OTHERS ARE INTIMIDATING

It can be hard to feel comfortable, much less free, in your job when someone on your team is inconsiderate, critical, or intimidating. The first thing to remember is not to take it personally. When others fail to create emotional safety, it's usually a sign that they are distracted, anxious, or troubled in some way. Below are some suggestions to move toward a relationship of greater trust.

Break the Ice: To build familiarity, make a point of greeting others or making a verbal or nonverbal connection on a regular basis, in a brief and simple way. A casual "Good morning" may be sufficient.

Express Support: This will likely feel counterintuitive, but expressing support verbally or asking how you can specifically support a manager or coworker can begin to break down the walls. Try "I want you to know that I'm here to support you on this project" or "What can I do today to support you?" The answer may surprise you. Be prepared to follow through on your offer, even if it falls outside of your job description.

Stay Calm: It may not seem fair, but often the best thing you can do with an inconsiderate supervisor or coworker is to remain nonreactive, and to keep your own internal state calm. This subtly invites the other person to calm down as well, and keeps your own mind clear to speak and act with integrity.

Ask Around: Ask other people about their own experiences with the person you're struggling to connect with. A wider context can increase the sense of familiarity and raise your capacity for empathy and understanding.

Start the Ball Rolling: If there's something you want in your job, or something you think is a good idea for the team, it may be possible to initiate it without explicit direction or approval. Rearrange the furniture in your office, or speak to someone in another department about your concept. Your initiative could spark others' interest.

PART II:
COLLABORATION

"Follower is not a term of weakness but the condition that permits
leadership to exist and gives it strength."
Ira Chaleff

A t this stage of development, dancers are familiar with a wide
range of dance vocabulary, and are able to navigate the floor
comfortably, responding to basic rhythms and phrasing in
the music. They change partners often, and welcome every dance
as a distinct exploration bringing its own surprises, challenges, and
thrills. Do you take a step softly, or with a sharp accent? Do you
embrace your partner tightly, or gently? Social dancers strive to be
able to partner—to successfully collaborate—with anyone, and this
can be a powerful approach to work as well.

Just as a dance shifts from moment to moment, a professional
project can change unpredictably from week to week or month
to month. Our collaborative relationships, whether in dance or at
work, require commitment and dedication, because no one knows

for sure exactly what's coming next. On the dance floor, two steps backward don't necessarily guarantee a third. A new partner might react differently to the same approach you used successfully with a familiar one, and the same is true with our colleagues' words, actions, and reactions. In order to work together over time, we need to be able to show up and do our part. But we also need to be able to adjust to one another's personalities and styles as much as we do to changes in logistical circumstances.

Skillful collaboration allows a team to produce, invent, develop, and achieve more than any one person could on their own. It is the fundamental reason we come together at work in the first place. Whether you work in a team of two or in an organization of thousands, smooth day-to-day collaboration is key to both personal and professional well-being. We need one another in order to do our best. The skills in this category help you to establish healthy and sustainable work rhythms with others.

Think of collaboration in a broad sense, from the smallest conversation to the most complex project. Whether you are in the same room with others or working remotely, you are still united by a shared goal. In this part of the book, you'll explore ways to build effective professional dialogue with others through four skill pairs: structure/delivery, expectations/boundaries, adaptability/flexibility, and decisiveness/presence. These four skills build on a foundation of connection to help you express the strength of the following role, take ownership of your work, and reinforce mutual accountability with leaders. As in part I, the leading skills are listed alongside the following skills so that you can see how the two roles complement one another.

Generally speaking, the leadership role focuses on the big picture, and the followership role focuses on the details. In strong collaborative dialogue, however, the two roles may seem to overlap and become one effort. Where followership manifests in technical expertise, skills, and what it takes to do one's own work well and consistently, leadership is the coordination and management of the collective expertise and skills of many people. Because we all must self-organize our work days to some extent, it is not difficult to see how we actually lead ourselves through our day. It's our inner leader who makes a to-do list, sets a morning routine, and keeps an individual filing system.

Similarly, even official team leaders and supervisors often distinguish between management activities and their own work. When they speak of the latter, they are referring to the followership aspect of their job. No matter where you find yourself in the hierarchy of your organization, you are most likely alternating between leading and following roles throughout your day. Begin to notice when and with whom it makes the most sense to lead and when and with whom it makes the most sense to follow.

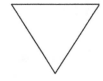   

LEADING SKILLS   **FOLLOWING SKILLS**

STRUCTURE   **DELIVERY**

EXPECTATIONS   **BOUNDARIES**

ADAPTABILITY   **FLEXIBILITY**

DECISIVENESS   **PRESENCE**

QUESTIONS TO GET STARTED

1. What does successful collaboration look like and feel like to me?

2. How might my team or organization benefit from improved collaboration?

3. What do I perceive as my biggest obstacle to collaborating more successfully?

CHAPTER 4:
STRUCTURE AND DELIVERY

STRUCTURE
+
DELIVERY

The Leader's Role: Organize collective work

Looks Like: Maintaining and coordinating calendars, project plans, agendas, and deadlines; arranging for physical setups, equipment, and resources; delegating appropriately

Benefit: Keeps your own schedule clearer and calmer

Impact: Enables others to work efficiently and sustainably, optimizes productivity

When It's Missing: Confusion, miscommunication, redundancy, misunderstanding, urgency, missed deadlines, low productivity, low quality

---

s part of their common vocabulary, social dancers reference basic geometric shapes. Lines, circles, and triangles form paths of movement for each individual dancer and for the couple as it travels around the dance floor. This spatial navigation system helps leaders and followers to function as a team. As described in chapter 3, the leader is responsible for guiding the follower securely along these pathways. This basic structure is not only necessary for safety; it also sets the stage for creative exploration. To that end, the leader is also the master of time, offering precise cues that correspond to rhythms, accents, and musical phrases.

In our workplaces, too, team leaders seek to manage space and time in ways that are conducive to professional success and creative problem-solving. Open floor plans, conference rooms, site assignments, and telecommuting are all strategies to optimize the structure of work in space. Similarly, deadlines, schedules, and project plans are ways of structuring work in time. Managers and supervisors customize these guidelines based on the goals of the team and the needs of its members. Some jobs have strict working hours and are tied to specific locations; others are flexible and can be done remotely.

J runs a construction company with a team of over twenty tradesmen representing a variety of different specialties. He says what makes his business successful is that he gives his workers a lot of freedom in the projects they work on, because there's just no way for him to keep track of everything. Here's how he describes the relationship with his crew: "I have one guy who handles details that take more time and would be overwhelming for me. When others need to leave early or come late, they all go to him. He's like a project manager, and if he can't find a solution or doesn't know the answer, he will call me at the end of the day. For electrical, plumbing, and materials purchasing, I have another guy who coordinates the individual trades who do that work. He takes care of that, and if there's something unusual, he'll let me know. I tell them all what projects need to be finished at certain times, and we talk through who should go where and when so that we can get all the projects done."

Note J's references to both space and time in devising an informal yet multitiered structure for his team members to work within. There's a casual note of confidence in his voice as he describes the flow of communication. Supervisors like J are very familiar with the field, industry, and area of knowledge covered by their team's work. But it's not only technical expertise but also the ability to orchestrate projects from beginning to end that makes for effective leadership. Without enough structure, employees won't know how and when to focus their energy. Too much structure, though, squashes creativity and initiative.

On one end of the spectrum, an aversion to being overly controlling can result in loose planning, leaving teams adrift and confused. On the other hand, fears of losing control can result in micromanaging, which interferes with the flow of work in a different, equally frustrating way. The loose planner resists either leading *or* following, while the micromanager tries to do both at the same time. Both of these patterns are irritating because they make it difficult for others to work with us. They shut down collaboration by blurring the two roles.

The remedy is in recognizing that it's not control but connection that works. Leaders who practice the skills in part I of this book—clear communication, commitment to an inclusive atmosphere, and sincere caring for the well-being of others—are much better able to create functional systems for the people who work within them. Ideally, organizational structures neither restrict nor overburden workers, but rather provide a healthy balance of creative freedom and accountability.

J told me this story of how his team averted a major setback by leveraging their own balanced system of working together: "When we started running the pipes, my electrician pointed out that we needed to separate certain pipes by twelve inches and that the other guys [from a different contracting company] were not doing that. It would have caused a lot of problems, and it wouldn't have been up to code. We would have had to start all over again. I had completely forgotten about this detail, and the plumber didn't know about it either. Because my guy was paying attention, we caught it early." Since J consistently communicates with them as equals, many of his employees have organically developed both leading and following skills. They can work independently, direct others, and also defer to J when a question arises. The dual nature of their roles reinforces a high level of trust in their relationships and guards against potential errors. This story is also a great illustration of a healthy dynamic between expectations and boundaries, the subject of the next chapter.

The Follower's Role: Execute individual work
Looks Like: Meeting deadlines, producing quality work, identifying problems and addressing them proactively
Benefit: Demonstrates expertise, reliability, and value; increases sense of accomplishment and job satisfaction
Impact: Frees others to focus on big-picture strategy
When It's Missing: Procrastinating, missing deadlines, partially completed work, losing track of information, making the same mistakes repeatedly, deflecting responsibility to others

---

The follower's view from the dance floor: *You spiral abruptly to the left so that your hips are facing outward, just beyond the leader's right thigh. You exhale and soften your right shoulder and elbow to keep your touch light and relaxed. Contracting your leg muscles, you take small, quick steps forward to match a rhythmic line in the music, flip your hips the other way, and take one long step to land back in front of your leader, unwinding into a neutral posture and balancing on the ball of your left foot. You release the tension between your shoulder blades, and adjust the curl of your right fingers in your leader's hand as you mirror her side step. She abruptly turns again, this time in the opposite direction, and you twist to the right. But before you can advance, you feel the inside of her shoe touch yours: a* parada.[17] *You pause for a split second, lifting your left foot a few inches off the floor, sliding it along your own inner calf, and placing it down neatly on the other side of your leader's foot.*

Advanced followers of social dance appear to move effortlessly, but in reality, they are continuously making dozens of subtle, unseen adjustments to keep the flow of the dance going. With every step, a dancer aligns ankle, knee, hip, and shoulder joints, controlling the shift of her body weight from one foot to the other at an even pace. She concentrates her center of gravity by engaging the abdominal muscles, and draws her legs together while swiveling to minimize any drag or delay, balancing on the ball of the foot when rotation is required. Based on the tempo of the music, she creates a predictable step size and positions herself at an optimal distance from her partner. The greater the follower's mastery of technical execution— her ability to deliver timely, reliable, and consistent movement—the freer the leader becomes to invent complex and fluid sequences for the couple. However, if she is not proficient, the opposite is true: the team's options decrease, and the dance becomes more rudimentary.

On the dance floor, leaders compose steps and sequences in a particular order so that followers can perform them comfortably and well. At work, organizing structures like timelines and project plans do the same thing for groups of people. But the skill of completing good work within those structures is often taken for granted. In fact, it's a measurable proficiency in itself. Part of a manager's job is to coordinate multiple interconnected pieces of work through schedules and deadlines. In environments where hundreds or even thousands of people are involved, we sometimes forget how much our work impacts others.

---

17   A decorative element in which the leader creates a pause in the dance, placing one foot in contact with one or both of the follower's feet, usually inviting him or her to step over.

REALMS OF RESPONSIBILITY

Responsibility for managers and team leaders lies primarily in the macro-realm of planning and coordinating, whereas individual team members carry equal responsibility in the less-visible micro-realm of execution, where the work gets done piece by piece every day. If the small details aren't completed, the final product will never be realized. The micro and the macro function together or not at all. Team members must take full responsibility for their own tasks in order for the team leader to orchestrate the bigger picture.

In highly collaborative teams, many people—perhaps everyone—may be involved in the leadership activity of structuring the work. Yet, delegating or assigning tasks can only maximize productivity when individuals commit to those tasks and get them done in a predicable amount of time. This is sometimes what is meant by *taking ownership* of a certain aspect of a project. Missing calculations can be the reason that an entire engineering team fails to complete a system update. An incomplete data set might be the reason a research experiment has to be redone. Delivery is not an inborn ability or a personality trait, but rather a collection of self-regulation strategies that we refine over time.

We may ask for guidance or resources, but ultimately we are responsible for getting our work done. It takes focus and stamina, and a willingness to let go of personal opinions and accept someone else's direction. If some of us are unable to deliver, others will need to step in, draining energy away from other areas and sometimes tempting supervisors to micromanage. Some supervisors micromanage because of an inability to delegate, but we can unknowingly encourage this same behavior if we fail to inspire their confidence.

V was laid off from her job as a marketing analyst and took an entry-level position in a different industry. Used to working independently, she soon became frustrated under the direction of a well-meaning but inexperienced new manager. She recalls, "We were always bickering. I would question all of her decisions and blame her for everything. I didn't have much respect for her and thought she was a bad leader, so I would resist everything she asked me to do. I think that made her start micromanaging, which was even worse."

When V learned about the concept of followership, however, things began to change. She continues, "I remember the week I got back from a followership training. I was pretty excited to present these new ideas to the manager, but she was super defensive. Instead of pushing it, I stepped back and let it go. I realized that my behavior had been threatening her, and I started seeing things more from her side. After that, instead of arguing, I would just do what she asked me to do or ask for clarification. It made a big difference. She started showing up more as a coach rather than trying to force me to do things." V realized that even though the manager was far from perfect, she herself was in a position to take action and influence the relationship for the better. As soon as she focused on doing the work and accepted the manager's decisions, the micromanaging stopped.

Managers and supervisors experience anxiety and insecurity just like the rest of us. When we recognize and empathize with them, they are better able to cope with their own stressors, whatever they may be. In addition to discomfort with authority, like V, employees at all levels may also struggle with procrastination, distraction, and overwhelm. Regardless of title, most of us need some kind of stress-management strategy in order to maintain a healthy work rhythm. In the context of a team, we can also help minimize that stress for others. Ask yourself these self-assessment questions:

How do I confirm what tasks or projects are my responsibility?

In what ways do I demonstrate that I am taking responsibility for my work?

In what ways do I contribute to structuring my team's work, when appropriate?

MINIMIZING OVERWHELM

Overwhelm is an extremely common experience in our workforce. We are all chronically busy, and the labor system we live in tends to ask for more and more. Yet, the difference between feeling overwhelmed by work and feeling engaged by it can be partly a question of perspective. How do you internally react to what managers, coworkers, or institutions ask of you?

K is an architect who runs her own business, and, at the time we met, she was also working part time for another design firm. Organizing her time to both keep up with her boss's timelines and address the priorities of her own clients was a major challenge. She felt totally overwhelmed, and was skipping lunches and suffering from physical and mental exhaustion. I knew K as a passionate artist with an impressive portfolio, but none of her current projects inspired her.

When she became my client, she made a commitment to eat lunch every day. This seemingly small act of self-care was, in fact, not so small, and immediately gave her more energy. Then we took a step back to reflect on her two jobs. Is this really what she wanted? Were the expectations realistic? As K sat with these questions, the truth surfaced: Her dream was to work for herself, and she had only taken the part-time job out of fear that she wouldn't be able to attract enough of her own clients. But a year into this arrangement, the opposite was true—she actually had a full client load in her own business and was *still* working three days a week for someone else. Once she saw this clearly, she realized it was time to leave the other firm. That transition would take time, though, so we still had to put some strategies in place to keep her centered and able to manage the workload.

K implemented a new scheduling system and renegotiated some deadlines, but most importantly, she chose a different inner perspective. Rather than seeing herself drowning in the work, she saw herself calmly paddling across the water in a canoe. The image was a powerful one, and gave her the strength and focus to keep going until she could focus completely on her own business and scale back on her work hours.

Reflect on your particular work situation. Where or when do you tend to feel overwhelmed? When do you feel out of control, as if there's way too much for you to do, understand, or respond to? The next time it happens, try these three strategies, the same ones that K used in our story, to shift out of the illusion of victimhood and reclaim your power of choice.

One Small Thing: Self-care isn't optional; it's mandatory, especially if you live in a society like ours that seems to encourage overwork and isolation. To reduce overwhelm, we need to remember that we are humans first and workers second. Practice self-care by doing one small thing to center yourself in your body when you start to feel overwhelmed: listen to your favorite song, make a cup of tea, take three full breaths, or create your own simple ritual.

Get Realistic: Are you asking too much of yourself? In some organizational cultures, unrealistic expectations have become normalized. More is not always better or possible, and overwhelm can lead to costly mistakes and personal illness. Take an honest look at what you're expecting yourself to do, and consider whether it's actually realistic. If it isn't, how can you adjust your workload to be more sustainable?

Choose a New Perspective: Our inner state mirrors our outer circumstances, and each can influence the other. When you take charge of your inner state, you reclaim your power to impact the world around you. No matter how demanding the external circumstances, you can always choose to shift your focus. You can use a symbolic image like K's canoe to shift your perspective, or select a memorable phrase instead. Here are some examples:

I choose to focus on one thing at a time.

I choose to feel grateful that I have this job.

I'm doing the best I can, and I choose to believe that's enough.

Even if everything isn't done perfectly, I choose to believe it will be okay.

ADDRESSING THE INNER CRITIC

Many of us have an inner critic—that voice of doubt, judgment, or skepticism that appears when we speak or act outside of our comfort zone. Sometimes new situations or people trigger the inner critic to pipe up and remind us that we're not clever enough, not prepared enough, will surely fail, or maybe don't deserve an opportunity we've been given. The critic is a frequent underlying cause of both procrastination and perfectionism, patterns that prevent work from getting done. Together with a practice of offering yourself self-compassion, the practice of *witnessing* the critic can soften its edges. Witnessing is a kind of calm, nonjudgmental observing, as though from the back row of the theater of your mind. Many contemporary mindfulness practices encourage a similar perspective. Try this brief exercise, inspired by the work of coach and trainer Amy Lombardo:[18]

1. Mentally step back and observe the critic. Give it your full attention.
2. What is the critic really saying? Or what would it say if it could speak?
3. What sensations or emotions are present in your body when you hear that message?
4. If sensations or emotions are present, gently let them go with a few long exhales.

This kind of awareness-building may not eradicate negative thoughts completely, but it is a powerful first step. Witnessing puts some metaphorical distance between you and the critic. With that distance, it's easier to see that the voice is not necessarily the truth, but rather just one point of view. You can begin to question the function of this voice in your life, its origin, and its validity. It may start to feel less intense, or less absolute.

---

18   Amy Lombardo is the author of *Brilliance* and founder ofBrilliance Academy for Personal Transformation and Social Change.

PRACTICING DELIVERY

Getting your work done probably sounds like an obvious part of your job, but there are a variety of reasons it may be challenging, even if you have the best of intentions. If procrastination, perfectionism, or distraction ever get in your way, these strategies may help.

Plan Ahead: If you're working on deadline, be conservative in your estimates and aim to finish early. Then, when the inevitable curveball appears, you'll have time to adjust.

To-Do List: Update your list daily, first thing in the morning, and prioritize it based on level of urgency. Make sure every item on your list is specific and actionable. This reduces your cognitive load and removes some of the time and effort of decision-making, which you only have a limited capacity for each day.

Review:[19] Take a moment at the end of the week to review your own work. Schedule it into your calendar at the same time every week. Did you complete everything on your list? Are some upcoming deadlines more sensitive than others? What are the priorities for the next week?

Eliminate Distractions: This often seems like a losing battle for many of us, but simple changes such as closing a door, wearing earbuds (or taking them out), or turning off the internet for periods of time can give you an extra productivity boost when you need it.

Frequent Breaks: Studies show us that many short breaks are better than fewer long ones. Set a timer and give yourself a five-minute break every twenty-five to thirty minutes to keep your mind fresh. When you take a break, stand up, stretch, or move your body in some way.

Get Help: If there's something you're not sure you can handle

---

19   In productivity consultant David Allen's *Getting Things Done*, the review represents the *reflection* phase of a five-part organizational system. Allen's five parts include *capturing, clarifying, organizing, reflecting,* and *engaging.*

on your own, don't wait to get help with it. Remember that one of the reasons we work in teams and companies is so that we can help each other get the work done.

Avoid Perfectionism: Perfect is the enemy of good. If you find yourself revising excessively, or redoing some part of your work over and over again, check in with yourself. Is the desire to do it perfectly sabotaging your ability to finish? If you must, ask someone else to check your work before submitting it, but don't get stuck in the loop of perfectionism, which can eat up your valuable time.

WHEN OTHERS ARE DISORGANIZED

It can be a struggle to deliver when others aren't clear about what they want or have trouble coordinating their work with yours. Vague direction or, on the other side, micromanaging may have little to do with your performance and more to do with a manager or team leader's own challenges in letting go, trusting, or delegating. This may be especially true if the supervisor used to fill the role you are currently in. As annoying as it can be, try not to take it personally. Here are some suggestions for how to respond:

Confirm: Confirm in advance both the work to be done and also the date it is due. Repeat this information back to managers or team leaders in their own words, in writing if appropriate. This can help others see that you are committed to the work and that they can trust you to complete it. Confirming also holds both of you accountable for the agreement. Consider the following examples:

"I'm confirming that I'm going to revise parts *a*, *b*, and *c* of the report. Is that correct?"

"I'm confirming that Mary and Robert will continue developing part *a*, and that Lucia should take over parts *b* and *c*. Is that correct?"

Check In: Take the initiative to check in with your supervisor on the direction of your work. If he or she has difficulty coordinating or delegating, it may be helpful to track your own contributions to specific projects on a regular basis. Asking questions and identifying the moving pieces can encourage more understanding and decisiveness.

Delay Your Response: If the other person is micromanaging by phone or email, try waiting a little longer than usual before responding. If you are concerned that this might provoke a conflict, ask for uninterrupted time to work so that you can do your best, and ask whether you are needed for anything specific during that time.

CHAPTER 5:
EXPECTATIONS AND BOUNDARIES

EXPECTATIONS

+

BOUNDARIES

The Leader's Role: Articulate values

Looks Like: Establishing standards of performance, safety, and ethics, and a system for upholding them; stating the purpose and scope of projects; identifying desired outcomes

Benefit: Produces smoother and more successful plans, timelines, and deliveries; ensures ethical practices and behavior

Impact: Empowers others to align with common values

When It's Missing: Lack of integrity, low standards, corruption, abuse

---

There is an urban legend in the tango community that goes something like this: In the moment followers step into the arms of their partners, they know everything about the dance to come, even before taking the first step. What does this mean? Is it the leader's posture and muscle tone, the shape and pressure of the embrace, or perhaps the invisible electromagnetic field around the body that sets such a strong expectation? Is it our mirror neurons that tell us what values the other body is silently expressing in the moment?

In classical tango technique, the leader holds the artistic vision of the couple, like a theater director. The follower is the actor, shifting like a chameleon from one partner to another in order to bring a story to life. Each story—or each dance—carries with it not only a physical shape and tone but also a set of assumptions about the world that it gradually reveals to the audience. In the same way, professional expectations refer to the trajectory of each project or program and also to the organizational culture in which we conduct our work: our professional world. Leaders set the tone for the working environments we all share. Individuals can sense when the tone is restrictive or corrosive rather than healthy and sustaining.

More powerfully than any official company policy or handbook, people feel our nonverbal signals. When we lead, we need to know what we stand for. Dancers take this quite literally, and train to express their values and their creative ideas through physical posture and gesture. Aspirational qualities such as confidence, honesty, and integrity are expressed through the body as much as they are understood in the mind. Through touch, dancers can feel the difference between a kind, respectful intention and a hostile, dismissive one. Similarly, employees can pick up on these signals in our body language, speech, and actions over time. The unspoken messages matter.

C worked in an administrative support role for a small educational nonprofit, where there seemed to always be way too much to do and not nearly enough time to do it. She soon noticed an inconsistency in the executive director's expectations of himself compared with his expectations of his employees. She recalls, "If someone made an ask of our organization, he was always really careful to manage our time well and make sure our needs as individuals were met, but he didn't model that with how he treated his own time. In many ways he was a great representative of the organization, but as staff members, we didn't need a leader who was totally overworked and underpaid and overwhelmed."

The imbalance in the director's expectations became exaggerated over time, and weakened an already fragile organizational ecosystem. As he continued to take on extra work for himself, C recalls, "We had this one employee who just flat out didn't complete their job very often. They didn't work forty hours, they didn't pull their own weight, and everyone just completely ignored it." Meanwhile, the impact of this employee's low performance began to threaten the integrity of the organization. Several of their educational programs failed to receive approval due to applications being submitted late or not at all. Programs that failed to receive approval, in turn, did not qualify for funding to keep them going.

Eventually, the problem was addressed in a daylong team retreat, and other members of the organization, both leaders and followers, were able to have an open and honest dialogue: "We talked about the needs of the team and how we can achieve those needs. Coworkers who don't normally speak up spoke up. We had volunteers speaking up. From my perspective it took a lot of courage for those people to speak up in front of leadership. And we came back to the office and it was like it never happened."

Wait. What went wrong? Staff members clearly set boundaries, and formal commitments were made. I asked C, who has since left the organization, why she thought nothing worked. "I think that our leader was just really conflict averse, and paralyzed by having to approach someone and say, 'This isn't okay.' Singling someone out was way outside his comfort zone. But by avoiding that, he was really impacting us all in a way that I don't know that he understood."

It's a crucial part of the following role to set boundaries when expectations are unrealistic or, in this case, when expectations are too low. Ideally, this dynamic of alternately setting expectations and boundaries is not a battle, but rather a conversation through which the team arrives at the best path forward. At the company retreat, it seemed like that path had been found. But collaboration is a two-way street. Both leading and following roles must be strong. In this case, the failure came on the leadership side. The executive director's unwillingness to enforce fair and equitable expectations lowered morale and caused lingering damage to the organization. C and several others soon left.

Expectations are built on agreements that leaders and followers have adopted in good faith. All members of a team commit to upholding the same standard of performance or code of ethics. As leaders, our side of the agreement is like making a promise to all who follow us, and our actions are never neutral. We either earn the respect and trust of others by upholding shared values and agreements, or lose it by ignoring them.

The Follower's Role: Preserve ethics

Looks Like: Refusing a task or suggesting alternatives when deadlines, assignments, or projects are unrealistic, unsafe, impractical, or unethical

Benefit: Maintains a sustainable workload and healthy working conditions

Impact: Helps others to establish responsible, realistic, and sustainable expectations

When It's Missing: Obeying against your better judgement, taking on more than you can handle, not being able to say no, burning out, permitting or enabling corruption or abuses of power

---

The follower's view from the dance floor: *As you complete the next turn, you catch a glimpse of another couple moving rapidly toward you from the edge of the dance floor. They're heading the wrong way. Your leader is facing away from them for an instant, and she signals clearly for a large sweeping movement with your left leg, directly in the way of the couple's advance. Even though dance floor etiquette says they shouldn't be there, they are, and it would be a direct hit. You slow your movement and sink into your right knee, keeping your left foot dragging along the floor behind you. You grip your leader's shoulder and pull your torso closer to hers by a fraction of an inch. You pause, holding tension in your arms. Your leader inhales sharply, but stays connected and then sees what you see, and the other couple brushes past her elbow, touching lightly but without incident. When space opens again a second later, your leader signals again, and you reach your legs out with extra energy into long, fluid steps, diving back into the flow of the dance floor.*

Dancers train to develop a keen awareness of how their own bodies move in space. They get to know their natural ranges of motion in major joints and muscle groups, identify individual strengths and limitations, and make necessary modifications due to chronic or acute injury. This familiarity with the physical instrument of the body allows dancers to respect the boundaries of what is possible and healthy, resulting in a comfortable, consistent, and creative dance experience both for themselves and for their partners. Importantly, the ability to communicate these boundaries to a leading partner (for example, by lowering an arm, taking a slightly shorter step, or verbally requesting a more open dance frame) requires that followers first identify and understand those boundaries themselves.

In this scene, the follower goes even further, preventing harm to both herself and others by slowing down her movement and delaying her leader's plans long enough to avert a potential collision. Generally, followers respond immediately and affirmatively to the leader's signals, a straightforward division of labor that makes social dancing functional, enjoyable, and creative for both partners. However, the follower must sometimes modify movements or literally stop moving if her own safety, or that of others, is at risk.

SETTING BOUNDARIES

We are used to the idea that managers and supervisors set parameters around the work that we will do. I think of setting *expectations* and setting *boundaries* as a paired set of responsibilities assigned to the leading and following roles, respectively. In practice, we all assert and negotiate the lines of expectations and boundaries in different ways and sometimes for different purposes, depending on our position. A team leader's expectations may be spoken or unspoken. Job requirements such as set working hours, weekly staff meetings, an open-door policy, or a quota system may be expectations that you take for granted as fixed and nonnegotiable. Other expectations may be specific to a project or to a certain role: that you will meet a deadline, that you will research certain products, that you will file certain reports, or that you will respond to customer calls.

A boundary, in the sense that I am using the term here, enters the picture when any of these expectations begin to interfere with the quality of your work, or with your safety or well-being as you do your work. This is incredibly important in any team or company, where your ability to do your work directly impacts someone else's ability to do theirs. The more moving parts and the more intricately divided the overall labor effort, the more crucial it is that you maintain healthy boundaries around what is possible and realistic for you to accomplish, so that everyone else around you can plan accordingly.

If you take on more than you can handle, or say yes to an aggressive strategy when you know it would be wiser to be more cautious, you could be putting an entire project at risk. The writing deadline you miss means that someone else can't submit the proposal on time, and the potential client may then choose another vendor. If you had set up the boundary in the first place, perhaps someone else could have taken on the writing part of the process, and allowed the proposal to go forward. The chain reaction can be quite dramatic. If a new supervisor expects you to sell product A to a hundred customers, but you know from experience that ten is a more realistic goal given current resources, the boundary might be communicating this knowledge in an informed and respectful way.

When R took the position of business manager at a small nonprofit, her supervisor almost immediately began asking that she work overtime without pay, attend evening events, take on additional last-minute tasks, and work offsite during her vacations. She recalls, "The amount of work was really overwhelming, and I think she was so used to doing those same things herself that it didn't occur to her that it was too much to ask. And because I was new, I really wanted to make a good impression and show her that I was valuable."

Beginning to say no to some of these requests, and to set boundaries around her personal time, required R to overcome her own perfectionism as well as the fear of losing her job. But she was exhausted and already starting to burn out. She knew the workload wasn't sustainable. Fortunately, once she decided to broach the subject with her boss, it wasn't as much of a conflict as she had feared. She writes, "I was genuinely surprised when I finally said that I didn't want to work during my vacation, and she agreed with me!" By honestly asking for what she needed one step at a time, R's communication with her director continued to improve, and became more of a dialogue around her workload and a revision of her job description. This shift prevented her own burnout and also helped the director establish a more sustainable long-term plan for the organization.

We ourselves are sometimes in the best position to understand what it takes to do our own work on time, and what gets in the way of doing it well. Whether your work is a product or service, clarifying what constitutes consistent and sustainable delivery is essential. If you discover that there are things you cannot or are unwilling to do, those also need to be expressed. The hours, deliverables, and scope of your work may be items discussed during hiring or predetermined by your job description, but at least some of these are likely to evolve over time. You discover what works by working. As you get to know your own needs, as well as your limits, you may need to draw and redraw the boundaries around your work in order to help the entire team function smoothly and sustainably.

IDENTIFYING THE NEED

Setting boundaries, of course, is not only for work—we all need to set healthy boundaries for ourselves in many aspects of our lives. Professionally speaking, though, I see boundary setting as a following skill because it primarily addresses the execution of individual or collective labor, whereas the leading perspective tends to address the organization of that labor. Different from expectations, which are typically set in advance, boundaries are maintained and communicated in the ongoing course of work, as what is realistic, safe, or possible shifts and changes.

For example, you may wish to set a boundary around the scope of a given task or assignment, or around how much you can accomplish given the external constraints of a project and the time available. Expectations and boundaries are a dialogue, each influencing the other to some extent. In strained work relationships, you may experience this dialogue as one person or team *making demands* and others *pushing back,* but in healthier ones it might look more like the two sides sharing perspectives and information in order to collaboratively refine the timeline.

When boundaries are not clear, your stress level is likely to rise. You may notice that you miss deadlines, skip lunch, and feel exhausted at the end of the day. Not only that, but because every individual's work is directly connected to someone else's, a lack of healthy boundaries around what is possible and sustainable can disrupt project timelines, budgeting, or client relationships when, inevitably, expectations are not met. You may also want to set boundaries in your life to negotiate a balance between work, family, and personal time. Agreements not to work on the weekends, lunch breaks, family dinnertimes, and date nights are all examples of boundaries that balance multiple priorities, helping to maintain a physical and emotional well-being. How do you know if you need a stronger boundary? Ask yourself the following:

When, where, or with whom do I really want to say no, but usually say yes anyway?

When, where, or with whom do I start to feel drained or tired?

When, where, or with whom do I tend to complain or feel resentful about "having to do" something?

When, where, or with whom do I long for more time to myself?

If these questions brought any specific situations to mind, spend five to ten minutes writing in a journal about them. Write freely without any censorship whatsoever. The first step in establishing healthy boundaries is identifying where you need them. This simple exercise may reveal some potential changes that could help you to work in a more sustainable way.

MOVING THROUGH HESITATION

The primary reason many of us have difficulty setting healthy boundaries at work is that we worry about losing our job, being passed up for promotion, damaging a relationship, or some other negative consequence. Although these concerns are sometimes well founded, they are often exaggerated. How can we evaluate our hesitation with more objectivity and speak up when it's important, even though we may still feel nervous? Below is a personal journal exercise[20] to help do that. *Note: There are times when your hesitation around setting a boundary may be fully justified. In the case of a verifiable threat to your personal or professional well-being, seek appropriate support from your community.*

---

20   Inspired by the work of Amy Lombardo, author of *Brilliance* and founder of Brilliance Academy for Personal Transformation and Social Change.

1. Acknowledge the Insight: The first part of speaking up comes before the speaking itself. It's when you realize that you feel overextended, uncomfortable, or otherwise in conflict with requests or behavior in your work environment. Or perhaps you see overlooked risk factors that need to be pointed out, analyzed, or accounted for. Whether the circumstances relate to professional interactions, work responsibilities, or the safety and security of a project, the moment when you realize something is wrong may be the same instant you begin to feel anxious. These feelings, somewhere on the spectrum between concern and terror, can make us forget the observation that sparked them in the first place. Give yourself permission to hold on to that initial observation, even if you aren't sure what to do about it yet. Remembering that the problem is outside of you (and not, by definition, *you*) may help you move through hesitation.

2. Name the Concern: When we explore anxiety, we enter territory that has its own logic, totally separate from the everyday, rational logic we are used to. That's because when we feel anxious, we're generally not using our minds fully. Fear and anxiety are manifestations of our fight/flight/freeze survival mechanism, and when that mechanism is triggered, a hormone called cortisol floods the brain and shuts down some of its higher reasoning. The more cortisol, the less reasoning.

If you're having difficulty speaking up about something that feels important, ask yourself, *What, precisely, is my concern or fear?* Naming the fear may already do much to dispel it. When we write down our concerns on paper or speak them out loud, it makes it easier for the thinking brain to see that its "logic" is not really logical. Be open to whatever the answer may be, however improbable or irrational. If you're having trouble naming the fear, try filling in the blanks in this sentence: *If I speak up about* x, *then* y—where y is usually an undesirable outcome. Just writing the fears down on paper can make them start to seem less intimidating and less inevitable. Consider these examples:

*If I tell them this vendor can't meet our needs, then my team will
be upset with me.*

*If I tell my boss I don't have time to do this extra report, then I'll
be fired.*

3. Evaluate the Concern: When anxiety or fear appears, it
removes part of the scene from view, like pulling a curtain halfway
across the stage. We literally fail to see whole parts of the situation,
like what we or others may lose if we don't speak up, or what potential
benefits may come to us or to others through our courageous action.
In the first example fear above, you may create a delay by taking an
extra week to find a new vendor, but if you stay silent and stay with
the old one, the entire project could fail, which is far costlier. In
the second example, consider which outcome is more valuable to
your boss: you saying yes and not delivering on your work, or you
being up front with your limitations and giving him or her the option
of getting the report done in another way? To quiet the emotions
and expand your way of seeing a stressful situation, ask yourself the
following questions:

What's missing from my perspective in this situation?

What other way might I look at this same situation?

What are potential positive outcomes of speaking up?

If I were guaranteed no negative consequences, what would I do?

4. Act from Your Values: There is no such thing as a neutral
stance, no matter the situation. Staying quiet or maintaining the
status quo is not a neutral choice. It is a choice to support the
status quo. Likewise, the choice to speak up is not necessarily a
choice to deliberately create conflict. It can be a choice to stand *for*
something, rather than *against* something. All of our actions—and
our inactions—count and have consequences.

Ultimately, you will evaluate decisions to speak up on a case-by-
case basis. No one can tell you what the right thing to do is, but you
can give yourself a powerful internal compass by deciding in advance

what's important to you about how you show up to work. Values such as honesty, clarity, and integrity can give you the courage to speak up about personal workload. Values such as dedication, commitment, and persistence may encourage you to speak out when project timelines are at risk. And values such as justice, equity, and inclusion may embolden you to stand up for unethical or unfair behavior or treatment regardless of the consequences. Strong values create successful teams and organizations. Ask yourself the following:

What values are most important to me as an individual?
What values are most important to my team or company?
What values are most important to my industry or community?
When I align myself with these values, what is my next logical step?

PRACTICING BOUNDARIES

For many of us, this skill is one of the most challenging to put into practice, because it tends to trigger the fear of losing one's job. Many of us are also conflict averse, and so we avoid conversations that are about differences of perspective, opinion, preference, or understanding. Ironically, the only way we can get back on the same page, so to speak, is by having those conversations. Here are some ways to prepare yourself for them.

Small No: Find one small thing you can say no to in your job—something that feels safe. Maybe it's as small as saying, "No thanks, no coffee for me today." It doesn't have to be related to your work. The idea here is to practice saying no so that it feels less scary and more normal for you to do so.

Interdependence: Recognize that to set a realistic boundary around your work is not an admission of failure or incompetence. Rather, it's an act that benefits everyone. Make a short list of everyone impacted by your work. Ask yourself what you could clarify for them about your own job that would make their expectations of you more accurate and sustainable. For example, "From the time I receive a request for a budget report, it takes me forty-eight hours to deliver it."

Anxiety Check: Make a list of all of the things that make you feel stressed or anxious in your job. If you have any individual people on your list, write out what exactly about your interaction with them causes you stress. For example, do you consistently struggle to say no to that person's requests for time or assistance? Then, categorize them by negotiability (100 percent required by your employer, possibly negotiable, and definitely optional).

Required	Negotiable	Optional
Starting work at 7 a.m.	Working overtime	Working weekends

For each item in the *required* category, list a reason the item might benefit you; for example, *Even though I don't like starting work at 7 a.m., I'm done early enough to spend time with my family, and I beat the traffic in both directions.* If this part of the list is long or if it feels overwhelming, it may be time to consider changing jobs.

Now consider the items in the category of *negotiable.* Imagine a change you could ask for that would make your overall workload more sustainable. How might this change benefit those you work with and for? For example, *I don't mind working overtime when there's an upcoming deadline, but I'd like to be able to work a few half days the following week. I know I would be much more productive if I had that recovery time.* With whom do you need to speak in order to negotiate this change?

Finally, consider the items marked *optional.* What level of stress are these items creating, and what is your reason for keeping them on your plate? Imagine a change you could make that would bring more balance into your schedule without sacrificing what is important to you. For example, *I'm managing sixteen accounts right now, and even though I enjoy the commissions, it means I'm working every weekend. I would prefer going down to twelve accounts, having weekends to relax, and being content with less income.* What do you need to affirm for yourself internally in order to act on this change?

Ideal Job: Describe your ideal workday from the moment you wake up in the morning to the moment you go to sleep at night. Include as many details as you can, even if they bear little resemblance to the job you actually have now. This is an exercise you can do anytime, no matter what your employment status. If you're seeking a new job, it can help narrow your search. If you are mostly happy with your job, it might bring your attention to smaller changes you can make that will make it even better.

WHEN OTHERS ARE UNREALISTIC

When others ignore boundaries, you may simply have to reassert them. The other person may have forgotten, may be distracted, or may not completely understand what is needed. If you think that your coworker or manager *does* understand and is simply disregarding your time or input on purpose, your response will likely depend on whether this is an isolated incident or a consistent pattern. Here are some strategies for negotiating the boundary line:

Indicate Capacity: Rather than saying no, point out the consequences of the request so that the manager or supervisor can make a more informed decision about how your time should be allocated. For example, "If I start this new task *A* today, I won't meet the deadline for project *B* tomorrow. Which do you consider to be the priority?" Sometimes others don't realize that asking you for more, or for something different, will derail other things that are already in motion.

Make an Exception: If your manager or coworker generally has realistic expectations, but once in a while asks for something extra, you may choose to make an exception. Be sure to verbalize that you are making an exception, so that your regular boundary is still clear. For example, "I know this is urgent, so I'm going to get this done in the next hour, but normally, I need a bit more advance notice so that I can be available at this time to take care of our customers."

Focus on Outcome: There are often multiple ways to achieve the same outcome. If you're asked to do something that doesn't seem realistic or advisable, try to learn the ultimate desired outcome of the task so that you can propose alternatives. Demonstrate commitment to the outcome while negotiating the specifics of how it will be achieved.

Assertive Language:[21] If you sense your perspective is not being heard or taken seriously, make sure you are using *assertive* language rather than *mitigating* language. Mitigating language diminishes the importance or urgency of a situation, and minimizes the perception of danger or risk. It is conditional, speculative, indirect, or diplomatic. Assertive language, on the other hand, is confident, forthright, firm, and emphatic. To speak assertively, affirm what you know to be true and in alignment with the values of the organization. In extreme cases, it may even be appropriate to interrupt. Consider the following examples:

---

21   Inspired by the work of Ira Chaleff, who provides a detailed exploration of setting boundaries on moral grounds in his books *The Courageous Follower* and *Intelligent Disobedience*

Mitigating	Assertive
I'm not sure this is the best approach to take with this client. There might be some other options to consider.	I know this client very well, and they will not respond well to the requirements in this contract. To preserve their goodwill and keep their business, we need to open a dialogue with them on this topic first.
I wonder if we might need to review some of the data a little further.	We need to look at the data more carefully.
Maybe we should rethink this course of action.	This is dangerous and needs to stop now.

CHAPTER 6:
ADAPTABILITY AND FLEXIBILITY

ADAPTABILITY

+

FLEXIBILITY

The Leader's Role: Revise plans as needed

Looks Like: Course-correcting or revising timelines in response to changing needs, new information, or unexpected events; reallocating resources as needed; willingness to try something different when things aren't working

Benefit: Allows discovery of multiple paths to reach your goals, and development of resiliency and strong track record

Impact: Allows others to adjust their work to meet real-time conditions

When It's Missing: Creation of unwanted or outdated products or services, wasted resources, failed projects or initiatives

---

On the dance floor, a major challenge for leaders is to adjust the couple's pathway of movement in response to the changing dynamics of the crowd. Because social dance is improvised, nothing is determined in advance. Space may suddenly open up or disappear in front or behind. Other couples may enter the floor at any moment. Although there is an established direction of dance (counterclockwise), other leaders cannot always be relied upon to diligently observe it. Beginners struggle with dance-floor navigation, frequently repeating the same step patterns over and over again even though doing so causes disturbance and disruption for others. As they expand their vocabulary of dance steps and gain more improvisational skill, leaders are able to choose alternative pathways to flow with and around other dancing couples safely.

As professional leaders, we must similarly adapt our plans to emerging trends and upsets, to unforeseen events, or to new client priorities. Sometimes these changes can be predicted in advance, but at other times they happen swiftly and without warning. *Adaptability* is the leader's complement to the following skill of *flexibility*, the macro to the micro. A flexible team supports new choices even when they are sudden or unplanned, trusting they are made with the team's long-term success in mind. With their attitude and general way of being, flexible team members can even encourage their managers or team leaders to assume more freedom of choice in making necessary adaptations to schedules, roles, and actual tasks. When we fail to adapt, we risk repeating the same strategy, making the same product, or maintaining the same system even though it is no longer working.

This was precisely the situation that M found herself in several years ago, when she became CEO of a social services nonprofit. She described a dwindling number of older volunteers who, although committed, were simply unprepared to address the rapidly escalating needs of the community they were serving. She explains the nature of the challenge: "Because our programs are complicated and expensive to run, we can't rely on episodic volunteers. We need people to work every day and run the programs [in order for them to have a real impact on children's lives]. That's a major challenge we face as an organization. It's very hard to get beyond the episodic-volunteer stage."

Tasked with coordinating the efforts of others, it's easy to stay in the same groove over time. It takes less effort to keep things going the same way than to adjust, revise, or update. Even when a product or service is no longer competitive, the momentum of old systems can make it feel difficult to change. But resisting change makes the organization rigid and its offerings obsolete. In M's nonprofit, traditional sources of funding were shrinking along with the volunteer base. Clearly, the old ways of doing things needed to change if the organization was going to survive. M needed to find ways to adapt quickly, and she did: "We started a family membership program—that had never happened before. Families can now do service work together, as a family. We had a family day of service to collect over 4,000 books, label them, and prepare them for giving. We had storytelling and a table for the kids to make bookmarks. It became a celebration of literacy. We've also been developing a young-professionals group. It's starting to really take off. The young professionals we've brought on, they're amazing, and it's spreading through their companies, so we're increasing our corporate giving programs. It has generated a whole new energy."

As CEO, M has faced her share of resistance from some longtime volunteers who were nervous about changing the organization's service model. In addition, the organization has many older members who are not comfortable with social media and digital technology. Even transitioning from handwritten forms to online registration was a difficult process. But she takes the long view on these new initiatives, and she's optimistic about the momentum they are already generating. She shared a story about one new member of the young-professionals group who not only inspired many of her coworkers to get involved, but ultimately got the attention of her company's founder, who came to observe one of the nonprofit's programs himself.

Soon after, he gave a generous donation that paid for the same programming to be executed at another school site. About her ongoing dialogue with the organization's staff and board, she says, "If there's no dialogue, there's no movement. We're all in it together. But I have to look at the long range and ask how we can contribute in the twenty-first century. I can't rely on what was done in the previous century." If we're too comfortable with outdated ways of doing things, we may actually believe that playing it safe is the best way to keep the business afloat, despite evidence to the contrary. The leading role can start to feel like a disciplinary one, a mandate to keep up the status quo. We can avoid this pitfall by redefining the role of the leader as *explorer* rather than *enforcer*. M's commitment to looking forward typifies the explorer archetype, and is what allowed her to guide her team through resistance and into a more sustainable and energizing constellation of community-based programming.

The Follower's Role: Adjust to change
Looks Like: Adjusting to changes in schedule, working conditions, or personnel; working beyond your job description; helping others
Benefit: Builds resilience, versatility, and stress-management skills
Impact: Helps others to course-correct and adjust priorities with precision
When It's Missing: Doing the bare minimum, feeling annoyed or irritated by requests, resisting change, becoming easily confused

---

The follower's view from the dance floor: *Abruptly you feel the signal to switch from a left to a right turn. There must be traffic on the dance floor, or else a sudden inspiration has come and shifted the leader's vision. Either way, you draw your ankles together for speed and pivot ninety degrees, releasing your lower spine into a spiral motion that moves you quickly from one side of your leader to the other. In the way that you hold your body and manage the flow of one step into the next, you create the possibility for decisions to materialize at the speed of thought. The lightness of your touch and precision of your step allows you to move in any direction at any time.*

Social dancers do not memorize choreography, but instead assemble movement sequences in real time. In order to do this, followers in particular train extensively for the mental and physical flexibility to shift in any direction, from any position, at any moment. In this scene, the couple responds to an unpredictable moment on a crowded dance floor, much as professionals regularly face unforeseen challenges presented by market dynamics, operational logistics, or political developments. Sharing the floor with dozens or even hundreds of other improvising couples, the leader must make judgment calls quickly. Followers who can respond to them smoothly and easily are the most respected, admired, and sought after in the dance community. They can dance well with anyone, and usually do.

Part of a team leader's job is to navigate toward the goal, and navigation sometimes requires changing course. In today's working environments, these changes are coming with greater frequency and abruptness than ever before, and we must be ready for them, even as they put us on unfamiliar ground. Just as adapting to changing external circumstances is an important macro-level leading skill, flexibility is a crucial micro-level following skill. When we're in the following role, we may resist sudden changes, in part because we don't always understand the reasons behind them. But failure to respond readily can hold the team back or negatively impact its target outcomes.

Flexibility asks us to self-regulate our own rhythm and style of working. Sometimes long periods of solitude are productive, and at other times collaboration is necessary to move forward. There may be aspects of your work that are physical and others mental, some portions that are organizational or administrative, and others that are creative or analytical. Being flexible means finding a way to keep moving regardless of the situation, and even learning new ways of working when your preferred routines are interrupted. You may be used to the privacy of your own office, but your new company has an open floor plan. You might prefer creative tasks but find that administrative tasks are part of your new job description. Being flexible means you are willing to do what is needed to help the team, company, or project move forward, even if what is needed is not always your first choice.

BEYOND JOB DESCRIPTIONS

When you're truly committed to your work, you aren't restricted by your job description. Be careful not to use it as an excuse to avoid helping or adjusting when there is clearly a need. Maybe you're an engineer but you're asked to meet with outside consultants for a special project. Maybe you're an editor, but you're asked to reformat the database so that the whole team can communicate more efficiently. Obviously, there are limits to how much extra work you can take on or how far you can step outside your expertise, but for short periods of time, being willing to rise to the occasion when help is requested can bring tremendous benefit to the organization and strengthen your own track record.

Having deadlines, targets, goals, and deliverables are all essential, but the truth is that there will always be times, maybe more often than we think, that someone will need a kind of help that isn't on the schedule, or that delays in the timeline make unplanned work necessary. By extending yourself at these times, you may be able to prevent a bigger problem, learn something valuable, or forge stronger professional connections.

T works as a program designer for an educational training company, and her division is made up of three separate but related teams. Through a rapid series of acquisitions, the company directives from upper management were changing frequently and abruptly for over a year. What kept her entire division productive during this confusing period? A commitment to helping one another. She explains, "We have a lot of remote workers and multiple offices, so we decided to have weekly videoconference meetings to keep everyone in the loop. A lot of us came from startup backgrounds or from professional development, so it was a pretty natural thing for us to do. I guess it sounds really simple, but no one else did it, and other teams ended up with a lot of problems simply due to lack of communication."

In those weekly meetings, T's team did a lot more than just keep each other up to date. They also aligned their language for communicating with clients, shared learning materials for consistency, and identified best practices for a variety of common client problems. Most powerfully, they established a cultural norm of helping one another outside of meetings, regularly stepping in to take client calls when other team members were unavailable, and sharing training resources to save each other time. The habit of mutual aid allowed them to excel despite massive upheaval in the greater organization.

What happened with the other teams who did *not* establish this kind of mutual aid system? T gives an example: "Well, in one case, a new software release was published without telling customer support. Clients panicked because their tools suddenly didn't work, and everyone was scrambling internally to get information so that they could respond to the flood of support calls. It was a mess." We could look at this situation and simply notice a lack of communication. That is true, but the underlying dynamics are more nuanced. Why weren't those other teams communicating with one another in the first place? T's theory: "The [development team members] just weren't thinking about how the release would impact the customer-support team. I think a lot of people just don't grasp the impact outside their own sphere." In other words, they were narrowly focused inside their own job descriptions. If they had considered their place in the larger web of their entire division, or had developed the habit of sharing information across teams, perhaps they might have been a little more flexible with their release date.

Expanding your idea of what you consider to be your job may feel confusing at first, but it results in a level of comfort with change that makes you more resilient in the long term. It saves time, because help is always there when you need it. In cultivating flexibility, you'll see options and alternatives more easily, whether working on your own or in a team. You'll be able to adapt and make progress under a variety of situations, including stressful ones, and support others in doing the same. Ultimately, you might see and pursue possibilities to work in different departments or even other companies that you may not have considered before.

WHEN TO ASK FOR HELP

Giving and receiving help is a fast and effective way to deepen professional relationships. If we're willing to *offer* help to others, we must learn to *ask* for help, too. No one can know everything, especially in environments that are continually changing. Ideally, a team's individual members represent a wide variety of knowledge, perspectives, and specializations. Working together smoothly, such a team becomes greater than the sum of its parts by weaving connections among these intangible assets. Excelling in the contemporary workforce requires an ongoing commitment to learn from one another and from each new challenge. Here are some clues that may suggest it's a good time to ask for help:

- You don't feel confident doing a task on your own or find yourself using vague language to explain your work.
- You are not certain you can meet a deadline, or you find yourself making excuses about missing deadlines.
- You don't know the answers to questions others ask you, or you find yourself dismissing or avoiding the questions.

In order to ask for help, we must accept that it's okay not to know something, and to open ourselves to the feelings of vulnerability that may come with that acceptance. No one is perfect, but everyone can learn and improve their skills. Unfortunately, many of us grow up stigmatizing asking for help, as though it were a sign of weakness. In her groundbreaking work on shame and vulnerability, research professor Brené Brown helps us to understand that many everyday actions that trigger discomfort—such as asking for help—are in fact opportunities to step into our courage. In *Daring Greatly*, she writes,

> Vulnerability is not weakness, and the uncertainty, risk, and emotional exposure we face every day are not optional. Our only choice is a question of engagement. Our willingness to own and engage with our vulnerability determines the depth of our courage and the clarity of our purpose; the level to which we protect ourselves from being vulnerable is a measure of our fear and disconnection.[22]

The truth is that asking for help or support is one of the most effective ways to build team cohesion and ensure success. We are designed by nature as interdependent creatures, built to live sustainably through an ongoing exchange of mutual support. When team dynamics reflect this inherent interconnectedness, everyone does better. Below are three suggestions for getting more comfortable with asking for help:

Normalize Interdependence: The myth of individualism has convinced many of us that no one should need help, that help is only for small children or for the physically incapacitated, or it's something you get only in life-threatening emergencies. Instead, what if it were normal to exchange support with those around us? What if this exchange, whether taking the form of time, expertise,

---

22   Brown, *Daring Greatly*, 15–16

or simply attentive listening, was a tide that lifted all boats, a continuous, multidirectional stream of pay-it-forward-ness? Asking for help might then become less personal and more general. The sweet potatoes are passed down the table, and the salad is passed back in the opposite direction. Everyone eats.

Build Your Community: Even if you know *what* to ask, you may not know *who* to ask. The way many of us work can be shockingly isolating. Even surrounded by thousands of others in the same building or in the same city, it's not uncommon to feel lonely. The remedy is to deliberately broaden your professional network. It's a lot easier to ask for help if you have a variety of people to choose from. Think beyond your own team to other colleagues within and outside your area or division, even outside your own company. Within a larger community, it's easier to see who can help with what, and to get the momentum of mutual support going.

No Is Okay: If you're going to ask, you have to be able to accept a refusal. And in order to be truly okay with a *no* response, you have to depersonalize it a bit. You're asking for something, but the answer is not an affirmation or a dismissal of your right to ask, nor is the answer a hint that you do or don't deserve help in the first place, which is how many of us are tempted to interpret it. Rather, the *no* is simply a reflection of a person's capacity, choice, and boundaries. The vast majority of people want to help if they can. A *no* usually just means, "I'm not able to help due to personal circumstances, resources, or priorities." Once we soften our fear of personal rejection or loss, it becomes much easier to seek support.

UNCERTAINTY

Uncertainty tends to provoke anxiety. When a project direction changes suddenly, or a big decision is made higher up the chain of command, you may feel nervous, angry, or afraid, to name just a few possibilities. Strong feelings tend to catch us off guard in our places of work, prompted by events that may otherwise seem ordinary. We can't ignore them, though: Sooner or later, neglected emotional material returns as a weakened immune system, depression, distraction, or disease. Squashing our feelings is, unfortunately, a pretty reliable way to create tension and conflict in our professional relationships.

The good news is that when we are able to witness our feelings with neutral attention, they start to feel less like a burden and more like a source of insight. We learn what's important to us, make clearer choices, and advocate for our needs more effectively. Here is a three-step process to make space for feelings around uncertainty.

1. Context: Bring to mind a situation where you have recently experienced or are currently experiencing uncertainty. In your mind, recall as many details as you can, including any other people involved. Are there concrete external factors causing the uncertainty? Is the uncertainty caused by a lack of information? Clarifying the situation can help expand your perspective and reduce anxiety.

2. Awareness: As your perspective shifts, note any internal changes in how you feel in your body. Does the new perspective bring relief, or does it make your feelings more intense? What story are you currently telling yourself about the situation? What assumptions are you making about yourself or others?

3. Inquiry: As you articulate your current thoughts, you have the opportunity to change your focus. How would you like to reset your perspective around this moment of uncertainty? How else might you interpret the situation? What do you know about your own strengths and abilities, or about your relationships with others, that could be useful now?

PRACTICING FLEXIBILITY

Even if you are used to taking on multiple roles or helping out with unusual tasks, the exercises below may strengthen your ability to be flexible. If you are not being asked to step outside your role very often, try switching up your own work habits throughout the week, and observe how it impacts your mood and productivity.

Say Yes: If you feel reluctant to help out when unusual needs come up, try saying *yes* without overthinking it. Trust yourself to figure out how you can help. *Note: If you typically say yes to everything and tend to take on too much, try saying no instead. See chapter 5 on boundaries for more suggestions on saying no.*

Compare Notes: Have lunch with a colleague whose job is very different from yours. Although you're not going to learn what they do in one conversation, the insights they share may inform your own perspective and make you more comfortable helping outside your field of expertise. Plus, showing interest in what others do builds connection and trust, something that encourages us to help one another.

Schedule Change: If you normally do one kind of task in the morning (say, correspondence) and a different kind in the afternoon (say, creative), try switching them around and see how the change impacts your energy and productivity. Experiment until you find a rhythm that feels balanced.

Venue Change: Try doing your work or arranging meetings in different locations (at home, at your desk, in a conference room, in a café, on a walk). Notice how these different venues impact your energy and productivity.

WHEN OTHERS GET STUCK

When other people get stuck on a challenge or resist asking for help, they may be assuming they need to figure it out themselves, or they may not want to feel vulnerable. Depending on the situation, these techniques may help:

Offer Support: If you have the sense that your manager or coworker is overwhelmed, a simple offer of help may make a difference. Make sure you indicate that you are willing to help with *anything*, not only tasks that fall within your job description.

Be There: If there's a way for you to work in close proximity with the other person, without speaking or interrupting, your presence may provide reassurance, and ease feelings of stuckness without words.

Something New: If you sense your team is in a holding pattern or can't seem to move forward, it might be useful to try something different purely for the sake of breaking the pattern. Invert a schedule, swap tasks, brainstorm "silly" ideas, or borrow a tactic from a different industry entirely. Choose something with a small time commitment and minimal risk to current operations.

Sounding Board: Offer to talk through a concern without a specific agenda in mind. Leaving the conversation open ended and encouraging your boss or colleague to verbalize thoughts can clarify what is needed and reveal how you or others might be able to help.

CHAPTER 7:
DECISIVENESS AND PRESENCE

DECISIVENESS

+

PRESENCE

The Leader's Role: Navigate toward a goal
Looks Like: Collecting multiple perspectives, considering what is best for the group, assessing timing, trusting your intuition, choosing the next logical step
Benefit: Lowers anxiety and frees up mental space for creative thinking
Impact: Allows others to move forward
When It's Missing: Delay, confusion, conflict

In social dance, the leading partner makes hundreds of decisions in a single three-minute dance. But how does decision-making, as a competency, influence a leader's relationships with followers? For dancers, it's not enough just to make the decisions when they're necessary. Leaders must be comfortable with the decision-making process itself, and manage it well. It must be seamless and organic, and it must feel easy and inevitable to all following partners. Leaders achieve this effect, in part, by defaulting to stillness, so that in the absence of a signal, followers recognize that the appropriate response is to wait.

At work, of course, decision-making is one of the most obvious and defining leading skills. The cascading impacts of decisions are one reason those with formal titles are paid more and granted higher status. Apart from the content of a decision, its timing is significant. Decisions in teams and organizations are often difficult to make, and carry tremendous weight at the highest levels. A quick decision that fails to consider all relevant data creates inconsistency at best and produces catastrophic loss at worst. Lots of these impulsive decisions create a kind of tunnel vision in which others are shut out of the process. Caught in this spiral, we can damage trust, lose clients, and make costly mistakes that impact everyone. Waiting too long to make a decision, another symptom of isolation, carries its own risks: missed opportunities, disengaged employees, general confusion and anxiety.

Nevertheless, every person in a leadership role must make decisions on a regular basis, and there is no such thing as perfect timing. There may well be multiple equally viable decisions, rather than one obvious right or wrong one. Since no one can predict the future, leaders must commit to working with whatever happens as a result of their decisions. The skill of decision-making can therefore be seen not as an expression of outstanding or superior judgement, but rather as a long-term process of navigating toward a goal, with many inevitable course corrections along the way.

The Follower's Role: Stay in the moment

Looks Like: Remaining calm under stressful conditions, working methodically through the details, providing consistent updates

Benefit: Allows you to experience ease, pleasure, and contentment in your work

Impact: Helps others to make timely, informed decisions

When It's Missing: Making mistakes due to rushing, failing to check work thoroughly, skipping protocols, failing to grasp the need for more information, panicking, jumping to conclusions

The follower's view from the dance floor: *Your leader has paused in an unusual position. Your right ankle is just barely crossed behind your left, your weight still balanced forward on the ball of your left foot. This song features a singer, and he's holding a high note while the rest of the orchestra is silent. Your leader isn't moving, but her body is relaxed and her arms are still. You soften your left knee and release the tension in your neck. You close your eyes and let your back heel drop toward the floor, enjoying the sensation of balancing in this rare shape, allowing a relaxed tilt in your right hip joint and lifting your left heel slightly off the floor. You breathe deeply, feeling the muscles in your back expand and stretch with each inhale, focusing on the beauty of the single note of the song.*

In a dance relationship, a follower rushing through a step causes discomfort and confusion for both partners. Jumping ahead before the leader signals breaks the balance and connection of the partnership and may also disrupt other dancers on the floor. Because the follower is nearly always stepping backward down the line of dance,[23] she is unable to see what is happening or where space might be available for the couple to occupy next. Because of this, a willingness to wait for the leader's signal is absolutely essential both for the dance partnership to function and for the dance floor itself to remain safe for the entire community. Through the practice of waiting, followers develop powerful presence.

In this scene, the leader has made a deliberate choice to delay at this moment, perhaps for safety, perhaps for artistic effect, or perhaps for another, unknown cause. In the pause, the follower's physical awareness increases as she lets go of any need to know what is coming next. As she lets go of the future, she becomes increasingly aware of the present, specifically the present-moment experience of her own body. She notices both the muscle groups that are most activated and the areas where she can consciously release tension. In this state of heightened awareness, the follower also provides something invisible yet essential to the leader: she continuously transmits her current position, or point of balance. This information reassures the leader and makes it possible to time the next decision with precision.

MOMENTS OF PAUSE

In a professional context, pushing ahead with an idea or a project without understanding the big picture can cause unnecessary conflict or provoke a costly course correction later. Efficiency is often associated with speed, but a timeline may require an unexpected pause or delay based on what is best for the team or company overall. Faster is not always better. There may be missing pieces that need to be incorporated before work can go forward, or a last-minute change that requires editing or revision. All of these considerations are part of the process, but in moments of natural pause, we can

---

23   By convention, traveling social dances such as tango move counter-clockwise around the dance floor. Dancers refer to this as the *line of dance*.

unintentionally pressure managers or team leaders to make rash decisions with a negative tone of voice or expression that comes from a feeling of impatience or anxiousness.

In contrast, simply being willing to remain present in the moment can calm managers and coworkers who may be under a great deal of pressure to adjust a timeline or integrate new requirements. And just as the dancer in the scene above makes sure her leader knows where she is, we can proactively make decisions easier for managers and directors by keeping them well informed during similar pauses, even if we don't always know what information will be relevant later. In fact, consistent informing and updating is a strategic proactive habit we can implement in the normal course of our work routine.

My client D, a marketing and operations specialist, was faced with a major test of patience during a particularly rocky period at a new tech startup. His manager, likely under a great deal of stress himself, was assigning D a heavy workload but also interrupting him several times a day. He writes, "My manager liked to drop by my desk frequently and seemingly without care or thought to my schedule or needs. I would allow him to interrupt because I feared that by asking for more privacy, it would ruin my relationship with him."

Even though the interruptions might have alleviated some of the manager's own anxiety, they reduced D's productivity and caused problems elsewhere. To D, it felt like a no-win situation. If he said nothing, he would fall farther and farther behind on his work, but if he asked to be left alone, he risked more conflict in an already strained relationship.

As an experiment, D decided to embrace the manager's frequent interruptions—literal *moments of pause*—rather than resist them. As soon as he accepted that the interruptions were going to happen, he started thinking of how he could be supportive in the follower role: "I decided that every time my manager would interrupt me, I would first take a deep breath and then tell him about what I was working on. An example of this would be 'Hi, Tim, I'm working on those social media ads you asked for. What did you want to talk about?' I noticed that this helped him gain a better understanding of my schedule, whether it was working with a deadline or a high-priority task. Even when it wasn't an important work item, I think it helped him gain more awareness of what exactly he was interrupting, because it resulted in fewer and fewer visits."

Directly asking for privacy might seem like a more obvious solution in this scenario, but that kind of request implies influence over someone else's time and space, which is actually a characteristic of leadership (see Chapter 4: Structure and Delivery). When you're in the following role, it isn't always the most effective choice, especially in stressful environments. The follower is most powerful when acting in the moment. D found a clever way to do this by providing relevant information that acknowledged the manager's concerns and simultaneously reinforced their leader/follower relationship.

This particular tactic may not work in every situation, but by choosing to embrace moments of pause, we get a clearer sense of what our options may be in relation to others or to our physical environment. Greater awareness helps us work more safely and intentionally, and to make subtle judgements about what is needed or not needed. Even in the case of a setback or an interruption, choosing to stay present lowers our stress response. We discover novel, and subtle, interventions that can shift the whole team toward a more peaceful and productive work environment.

SURRENDERING CONTROL

Organizational systems are marked and measured by time, starting with the hours we work every day and extending into longer chunks: quarters and years, project timelines, and launch dates. Organizing by the clock and the calendar increases our productivity, but it can also generate pressure and anxiety. Wherever deadlines, deliverables, and metrics exist, we will experience a sense of urgency from time to time, if not on a regular basis. Sometimes clients, supervisors, or board members will be impatient with us or our work, and sometimes we will feel impatient with them, with ourselves, or with some part of the process we do not have total control over.

Too much urgency depresses morale and compromises our communication with others. Like other forms of anxiety, it pulls us out of the present moment, and when we believe we're behind schedule or simply not fast enough, we think less clearly and make unnecessary mistakes. We may even freeze. We're less creative in general, and less able to focus. Learning to be present with yourself and with others is a process of accepting and getting comfortable with the unknown, and with a certain lack of control. There are many things we *can* control, prevent, predict, and solve for, but the conditions of our work are increasingly unpredictable, and there seem to be more and more new challenges, variables, and people throwing wrenches into our best-laid plans. The reality is that we have less control than we think we do, and that can be unsettling. Here are some suggestions to become comfortable in the gap between what you know and what you don't know:

Reality Check: How urgent is the request, task, or event that is triggering your feelings of urgency? Can it safely wait another day or another week? What truly needs your attention now? What part of the project is under your control? What can you act on now? Whatever you choose, give it your full attention.

Replace the *Shoulds*: At times, you simply don't know how long something will take. You may be waiting for your boss to get back to you with an approval, or you may be troubleshooting code or researching potential partnerships. Impatience often creeps in with thoughts such as *I should know how long this will take,* or *This should happen faster.* Replace the *should* with a more accurate appraisal of the circumstances. For example, *I don't know exactly how long this will take, but I can make a reasonable estimate.* Or, *This is happening more slowly than I anticipated. I can accept that, make adjustments,* *and let others know.* Accepting the way things actually are frees your energy and makes it easier to take appropriate action.

Trust the Process: When you actively choose to trust the process and the people involved in it, you relinquish the desire for individual, personal control. Trusting the process is seeing yourself not as an individual, but as part of a collective of people working together toward the same goal. The larger our collective, the less individual control we have. Collective time may appear to move more slowly than individual time, but it may also be necessary in ways that are difficult to see from the individual's perspective. Trusting the process also means believing that you will be okay, even if something takes longer than you would like it to.

THE ART OF UPDATING

Different from *engagement*, discussed in chapter 2, *updating* is a consistent way that team members provide on-the-ground details to those in leadership positions over time. This steady stream of information helps leaders to make confident decisions on a regular basis and keeps us calm by focusing us on tangible work. It also allows leaders and coworkers to feel our supportive presence in their lives. When we lead, we need to be able to communicate where we want to go. But when we follow, we need to be able to communicate *where we are right now.* Updating captures the point *A* that makes leadership's point *B* possible. Without one, we can't get to the other.

H, an experienced marketing director, likes to leave some time for open-ended conversation in all of her one-on-one meetings to encourage her team members to share anything they experience or observe from week to week. She writes, "Team members need to share, even when they're not asked for specific information, because you just never know when something *they* might know could become important. Those touch-bases are invaluable because that's where you learn those key tidbits about your business that you didn't even know were going on. Sometimes you get wrapped up in your own mind, and just like you have a high-level perspective that they don't have, they have knowledge of the details that you can't see. You could miss something really important if they are not able to communicate. Also, sometimes they can confirm your suspicions that something is off. Then you can fix whatever the problem is. It's not about blaming anyone; it's just about understanding."

H emphasizes that information *gathering* by managers and information *sharing* by team members are complementary activities. She explains, "The manager has to create an environment of trust, but the team members have to do their part. You can't expect a manager to spend hours and hours trying to gather information—the team members have to speak up. The two have to meet in the middle." What I find most striking about this story is that the team members themselves won't always know when they are contributing valuable information, or even what constitutes valuable information in the first place. Rather, it's the continuous habit of keeping her informed that matters. From that flow, she knows that gems will surface, even if she doesn't know what they will be in advance.

A director's job is to arrange our work around specific future goals and deadlines, but it's the everyday, sometimes mundane flow of information related to those goals that keeps the proverbial train on the rails all the way to its destination. In the following role, we sustain that flow by continuously providing details, questions, and observations about where we are in our work today. These updates, not only on technical progress but also on interpersonal dynamics and individual needs, enable team leaders and others to do the work of deciding where we'll go tomorrow. Ask yourself these questions to reflect on how consistently you keep others informed of where you are on a regular basis:

When or with whom do I tend to censor myself?

What types of information do I typically withhold?

What types of information might others want to receive from me?

PRACTICING PRESENCE

This skill may only be tested in moments of stress, but if you find yourself generally in a hurry to get things done, or if your work environment is chronically stressful and rushed, these strategies may help you enjoy your work more on a day-to-day basis.

Focus on Action: Place your attention on the physical aspect of whatever you are doing. What does it feel like to type on a keyboard, write with a pencil, or use a tool in your hand? What parts of your body can relax or be more at ease while you do the action? This may be easier to do with less analytical tasks such as filing papers or organizing your desk, but you can try it with anything for at least a few moments.

Write by Hand: Try doing some of your writing or drawing by hand. The mental effect of your hand working with a pen on paper is very different from what happens when your fingers are typing. You'll slow down and become more aware of your body.

Take a Walk: Breaks are important, but breaks that involve physical movement are among the most valuable. Moving resets your entire nervous system. When your senses connect with the environment, you feel safer on a gut level, and this allows your thinking brain to function better.

Gratitude List: Take one minute to write down everything you are grateful for in your job. No detail is too insignificant. Your coffee mug definitely counts, as does the fact that you have a job in the first place! Gratitude is one of the easiest and fastest practices to shift into a mental framework of contentment, and from there it is much easier to remain present with whatever the current circumstances may be.

Gratitude Challenge: If you're having trouble with a certain person or group of people, make a one-minute gratitude list about them specifically. This may be a challenge if you're feeling frustrated, but if you can do it, it's almost certain to shift your attitude and allow you to be more patient when you have to interact with that person or those people. If you can't think of anything, make a general gratitude list for yourself first; then try this one.

WHEN OTHERS ARE INDECISIVE

In order to make good decisions, the nervous system must be in a calm and relaxed state. Stress and pressure of any kind will impair the brain's ability to reason, evaluate information, and imagine possible scenarios. Therefore, one of the best things you can do for someone struggling to make a decision is to relieve the pressure they're feeling to do so. This sounds counterintuitive, but even a little bit of time can make a difference. Here are some strategies to try:

Give Space: It sounds simple, but just leaving the other person alone can be helpful. Even well-meaning, positive attention can be distracting. When we're alone, there is less for us to react and respond to, and that fact can make it easier to quiet the mind, reflect, and see more clearly. If you can reduce the noise level in the environment, even better.

Reassurance: Remind your manager or coworker that you have their back—that you will support the decision, whatever it is, and are available if talking through it would help.

Missing Pieces: Is there any relevant information, perspective, or possibility that is missing? If so, provide it in a direct and accessible form, but do not offer your own opinion on what the final decision might be unless you are in the role of co-leader in the situation.

Circle Back: Request a time to return to the decision point. An established container of time provides healthy accountability and can actually help others move through the process of decision-making without triggering unnecessary stress and anxiety.

PART III:
CO-CREATION

"We tend to believe that the leaders are in charge, directing and shaping followership behavior. Yet maybe leaders are malleable products of cumulative followership actions."
Robert E. Kelley

When dancers reach this phase in their learning process, they no longer look like anyone else on the dance floor. Mastery of the entire lexicon of the dance, as well as intimate knowledge of its musical canon, means that the tradition has seeped deeply into their bones. They improvise sequences and musical interpretations that have never been seen before and that others strive to emulate. The quality of their movement is what one of my early tango teachers[24] once described as "effortless, elegant, and efficient," and full of personality. They have made the dance their own.

---

24 Brigitta Winkler is a German dancer and choreographer. She has been teaching Argentine tango social dance throughout the United States and Europe since the late 1980s.

No matter what our line of work, most of us excel when we are encouraged to express ourselves creatively. This does not mean we must work in an artistic field—only that we allow our own strengths and ways of looking at the world to influence and inspire our daily tasks. I think of creativity as what happens when your intuition meets your intellect, as an integrated way of thinking that involves both mind and body, both conscious and unconscious awareness.

Some of us may have been taught that only leading is creative, that those in supporting roles are not integral to the process and are therefore disposable. Social dancers have a very different perspective. For them, creativity comes neither from leading nor from following, but rather from the alchemy[25] of the two. In social dance, there is no creation, only co-creation. Any team or company with strong connection and collaboration skills is on its way to becoming co-creative. It is the next logical step.

Indeed, our most innovative solutions in the work environment are the result of co-creativity, the fresh ideation that emerges from healthy relationships and ongoing collaborative work. These solutions can be potent and impactful even when small in scale: a new approach to managing client data, an updated outreach strategy, an unconventional partnership with another organization. At the industry level, creative teams are also the ones making the headlines: pioneering novel technologies to sequester carbon, testing life-saving medical devices, setting up networks of international microloans.

Creative problem-solving increases an organization's reach, supports the process of scaling up operations, and keeps teams working smoothly through times of transition and crisis. It can also correct systemic dysfunction, shift public opinion, and make our world more equitable and just. It is no coincidence that as both local

---

25 Alchemy has been documented as both philosophy and proto-science, known best for its aim of transforming base elements such as lead, mercury, and sulfur into what practitioners thought of as the purest element of all: gold. Metaphorically, alchemy represents any process that transforms two entities into a third. The alchemy of leading and following results in a tango.

and global challenges intensify, creativity is increasingly becoming one of the most coveted professional characteristics across all industries and sectors.

In improvised social dance, no two songs are ever danced in the same way. No two couples look alike from the outside, nor do dancers feel alike to one another in the way that they move and interpret the music. In many ways, dancers have normalized difference as positive and enriching, each individual striving to express the tango of their own body, and to appreciate the same in others. As such, the most successful teachers and performers are not revered solely for technical excellence, but for their distinctive quality of movement, or personal style—their co-creative skills. Attaining this level of expressiveness is a primary goal for many dancers, and it serves as inspiration to learn and improve beyond the basic and intermediate levels. Once the mechanics are learned, dancers don't want to move like anyone else. They want to dance their own dance. And this same desire, of course, is with us at work as well.

At this level, you may begin to sense that the leading and following roles in your team are more difficult to separate. When we are in creative flow with others, roles flicker and dissolve. The leadership and followership perspectives are sometimes experienced simultaneously, with and through our colleagues and work partners. As a team, when you brainstorm or develop a vision together, you are sharing a leadership mind. When you explore possible pathways or try something new in response to that emerging vision, you dip back into followership mode. When you are focused on potential in others or in the potential of the team, you are seeing as a leader. When you express your own creativity, you are the follower. Seeing is the character of the leader, doing the character of the follower. But in creative flow[26] states, seeing is doing and doing is seeing.

---

26   Psychologist Mihaly Csikszentmihalyi coined the term *flow* to describe a psychological state of absorption in one's current experience.

For highly trained social dancers, a leader's improvised choices are made possible by the following partner's ability to respond to them. Similarly, the follower can execute musically expressive sequences only to the extent that the leader is able to assemble them.

Still, as you compare the roles below, side by side, you'll notice that the following skills continue to focus on actions in the present, whereas the leadership skills focus on actions that point toward the future. This differentiation is equally necessary and powerful to achieve the creative tension of innovative problem-solving, even though your team may share leading and following roles more fluidly. These final two skill pairs, imagination/bravery and insight/style, open up channels for greater freedom, growth, and opportunity in

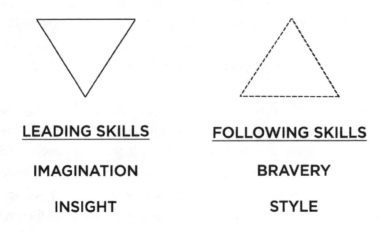

LEADING SKILLS	**FOLLOWING SKILLS**
IMAGINATION	**BRAVERY**
INSIGHT	**STYLE**

the course of everyday work.

QUESTIONS TO GET STARTED

1. *When or where in my work do I feel the most creative?*

2. *When or where in my work do I struggle creatively?*

3. *What do I perceive as my biggest obstacle to working more creatively?*

CHAPTER 8:
IMAGINATION AND BRAVERY

IMAGINATION

+

BRAVERY

The Leader's Role: Share your vision

Looks Like: Visualizing what you want to exist, asking what the world would look like if the problem were solved, dreaming, describing a vision of the future, guiding collective ideation

Benefit: Generates original ideas

Impact: Inspires others to commit to a shared purpose

When It's Missing: Repeating the same thing over and over again, short-sightedness, circular reasoning, cynicism

---

Imagination is the act of extending mental and emotional awareness into the unknown, into a world that does not currently exist. Our ability to do this with conviction allows others to take the same leap and then collectively reverse engineer the process of getting there from here. As Albert Einstein is often quoted, "Imagination is more important than knowledge." In *Cosmic Religion and Other Opinions and Aphorisms*, first published in 1931, he goes on to add, "For knowledge is limited, whereas imagination embraces the entire world, stimulating progress, giving birth to evolution."[27]

In dance, imagination is a felt experience, a knowing that a certain step fits here or a specific pause or rhythm belongs there. In professional teams, visions may be spoken, written, or seen, or may be cultivated in countless other ways. A vision may include or be entirely made up of a value system, a customer experience, a product feature, a concept of community, a system of governance, or anything else. Ideally, all employees contribute to the vision, and a director or team leader crystalizes it into paragraphs, diagrams, illustrations, or models. In whatever form the vision takes, it serves to align others with a common purpose, and it elicits the commitment that is required to move forward into the unknown and make it real.

I will never forget the first time I saw a man and a woman switch roles in a tango performance. It was only a few weeks after my very first tango lesson. Before then, it had never occurred to me that I, a woman, could dance the leading role in any social dance. Yet when I saw the performers exchange leadership and followership and back again, I felt a window open in my mind. Perhaps you have felt that sensation of neurons connecting, the infamous *aha* moment? For me, that three-minute performance shifted the entire course of my dance career—perhaps the entire course of my life. I realized that not only they, but also I, and anyone else who wished to learn, could play either role regardless of gender. I saw the possibility for a balanced and fluid sharing of power.

With this new vision, I was able to channel my effort, focus, abilities, and resources toward a more expansive, ambitious goal. My whole approach to partner dance training changed. Not only did I learn to lead myself; I taught other women to lead, and men to follow. I structured my classes and chose language that normalized the learning of both roles. All of this made it easier for others to do the same in the

---

27   Einstein, *Einstein on Cosmic Religion and Other Opinions and Apho-risms*, 42

communities where I lived and worked. Later, I created choreography for the stage that reflected my practice on both sides of the embrace. Because of the powerful vision of role exchange, I came to experience dance as a practice of empathy, inclusion, and mutual empowerment.

Visons are powerful, and they need not be modeled by actual people, as they were in my story, to have impact. A story told with conviction can disrupt an entire industry. Michael Margolis is founder and CEO of Storied, a strategic-messaging firm. In *Story 10X*, he writes, "If you want to unlock meaning and motivation with any audience, tell them a story that reflects the future they seek and identify with."[28] When presenting innovations that challenge the status quo, Margolis explains that it's essential to avoid the default *problem-solution* structure of communication, which only encourages wariness and skepticism.

Instead, we elicit far better responses from audiences by first narrating a powerful vision for the future, then shifting the perspective back to the present to identify any obstacles along the way. He continues, "You have an idea, a vision, a dream. Then, through a series of words and actions that spark the imagination of others, it can become a shared dream. And from there, it can transform from thought into a manifested tangible reality. This is how every great thing has ever been built."[29]

By swapping the genders of leading and following roles, the dance couple in my story offered a new narrative—not with words, but in the language of movement. It was a narrative based on equality, interdependence, and healthy power sharing. Because I resonated so strongly with those values, I began to support and contribute to the narrative in my own ways. Imagination is how leaders help us contextualize our work. It's that mental stretch into the future that makes it possible for teams to look *backward*, so to speak, from the future to the present, and plot new points on the map.

---

28   Margolis, *Story 10X*, 74.

29   Margolis, *Story 10X*, 74–75.

The Follower's Role: Take bold action

Looks Like: Self-educating to solve problems, seeking ways to expand knowledge and abilities, offering possible solutions to challenges, taking on tasks that are within your reach but new to you, taking initiative during slower work cycles

Benefit: Builds skill sets, develops capacity for different types of seeing, understanding, thinking, and contributing.

Impact: Helps others to dream bigger

When It's Missing: Waiting to be told what to do next, avoiding new projects or challenges, opting out of learning opportunities, stating problems without proposing any possible solutions

The follower's view from the dance floor: *You step around to the left, and your leader suddenly moves in, toward you, landing in the spot where you were standing only a moment ago. You feel the fabric of your leader's trouser leg brush against your shin as the two of you switch places. You step again, and again, spinning around the center, each time feeling that swish of air, your partner's stride barely glancing your shin bone. You twist fast, ankles glued together, and flash your foot up into the air behind you, then down again in the space of half a second. Spinning your hips around again, you see space opening, impossibly, behind your leader's back. But the leader's left leg is still extended across your path, offering only a small triangular opening for your step. You go anyway. The leg is suddenly out of your way, snatched inward at the last moment, and you spin again and cross your right leg tightly over your left, as though seated on an invisible chair. Unwinding, you step backward on a deeply bent knee and halt sharply on a percussive accent in the music.*

In this scene, the follower rises to the challenge of a fast and unusual sequence. She moves into unfamiliar spaces that at first seem impossible for her to reach. One characteristic of the strongest followers is this fearlessness. This willingness to literally step into new positions—even when doing so makes the follower vulnerable—allows the leader to see new ideas take shape in real time.

Pushing oneself to grow in this way, dance after dance, has a cumulative effect on the body of the follower. By developing muscle memory of hundreds of positions and sequences, the experience of trying something new itself becomes familiar. It is one quality that designates followers as advanced. Hesitation and second-guessing fade away, revealing the dancer's highly trained reflexes. The state of awareness is comparable to that produced by repetitive martial arts training. With this kind of highly trained follower as a partner, new movements or combinations are limited only by the leader's own imagination. Some of these new combinations may fail, of course, but most will succeed. With a more cautious follower, a leader never has the chance to try them at all.

At work, too, bravery is responding to a creative challenge with highly trained, if unprecedented, action. Often, that action must be taken without being able to predict the ultimate outcome with certainty or predict what additional actions may be required as a consequence of the first one. Informed by accumulated knowledge and expertise, acts of bravery can occur at any level of an organization.

Visionary leaders who paint a desired outcome in vivid brushstrokes make it easier for team members to creatively problem-solve in this way. Brave followers discover new paths when they know where they are going and are inspired to take the journey. What might be less obvious is that inspration flows in the other direction: brave followership can stimulate visionary leadership. When the destination is vague, a few ambitious steps in any direction can expose what's *not* wanted and sharpen the leader's focus. Followers who explore a variety of ideas well before the vision is clear can wake up the power of imagination in a leader who struggles to see possibilities.

Emerging from a strong foundation of active collaboration within a team or organization, acts of bravery shift us toward a rhythm of fluid following and leading with our colleagues and supervisors. The confidence it takes to develop an unconventional program or teach a new subject comes, in part, from knowing your director or leadership team believes you are capable of doing so. And likewise, a leadership team's vision is often inspired by its employees' willingness to chart new territory. At the co-creation level, following begins to feel a bit like leading and vice versa, just as the two halves of the yin-yang symbol visually dissolve into one other.

CREATIVE FREEDOM

No matter how specifically a plan is laid out by a manager or team leader, the implementation of the plan by team members will nearly always trigger new revisions or updates as the process unfolds. Those revisions then alter the team's next step, which in turn produces additional information to inform the next revision, and so on. This is the healthy cycle of creative flow.

When we approach our work with enthusiasm and commitment, we give managers and coworkers more freedom to do the creative work of developing current and future projects. To some extent, we give ourselves more freedom in the implementation of those projects as well. When in creative flow, a whole team might appear to be leading and following itself in a continuous feedback loop, but the individual members must divide the leader and follower roles and responsibilities amongst themselves, or alternate between them, in order to be at their most effective.

T is an engineer who solves large-scale technical problems in processing plants. He writes about a creative solution that came to him at a moment when an important project had reached an impasse, and as he himself was alternating between leading and following actions as part of a high-performing and well-connected team. He recalls, "It was Saturday night, around 2 a.m., and I was heading home from the office after a full day of running models and analyzing results. A large vessel had failed in a factory some days ago. Production had halted. The main question was whether the failure had been caused by something inherent to the process or if there was some kind of defect in the vessel. My team was asked to determine the answer by Monday. But our models were not developed to evaluate this kind of question with certainty. Our default plan was therefore to develop more refined models, but that was a weeks-long process, and we only had a day."

At this point in the story, T finds himself in a classic double bind. Based on what's been done before, he can either meet the deadline or solve the problem, but not both. But neither of those paths is acceptable; an original, unprecedented action is required. There is another path, but he can't see it yet. Overnight, perhaps while sleeping, his mind widens its perspective on the situation, and in the morning, a new path appears. He writes, "Sunday morning, over coffee and a croissant, the solution dawned on me. What if, instead of refining our models to capture the factory's existing process, we could do the opposite: tweak the factory's process to ensure that our models could predict its impact with certainty? By 3 p.m., I had developed a slightly modified process, one that we could confidently model. By 11 p.m., all of our tests showed it would work. We proposed it to the operations team Monday morning and they loved the idea. They implemented it within days and, indeed, it worked."

You may have experienced these kinds of *aha* moments yourself, when you suddenly see something you didn't see before. Although they may seem to come out of nowhere, they don't. In this case, T's creative leap was actually grounded in the hours of steady, diligent work that had been performed by his team beforehand. His story is a great example of how a foundation of strong collaboration makes breakthrough creative moments possible. T was fully committed to solving the problem and trusted his team's knowledge and expertise. He says, "In retrospect, we had studied this problem so deeply, and we had such thorough awareness of the capabilities and limitations of our own models, that the change in approach was less risky than it seemed at the time. What allowed me to deviate from the conventional approach was all the work my team had already put into understanding this problem."

Creative thinking thrives on a clear mind. Sometimes, a good night of sleep can provide this. At other times, a simple break in the work routine allows the mind to rest and expand its point of view. One way to increase the likelihood of breakthrough is to proactively investigate ways to make your team more cohesive on a day-to-day basis. Many strategies for this foundational work are suggested within the scope of the collaboration skills described in chapters 4 through 7. As T reminds us, his team had been exceptionally thorough and complete in their understanding of the problem and of their own tools, and that enabled his act of professional imagination/bravery.

CONFIDENCE

Creative work flows much more easily when we feel confident in our abilities, but new challenges of any kind, even good ones, can trigger our survival instincts and produce anxiety and doubt. We may know confidence when we feel it: perhaps a sense of relaxation and steadiness, or an inner certainty. But when we're feeling nervous, it's not always obvious how to find our way back to feelings of confidence. When we trust ourselves, though, we are much more likely to be bold and creative in our work, and so intentionally finding our way back to confidence is a skill worth nurturing. What can tango training teach us about this process?

Dancers practice confidence directly through the body, by cultivating healthy spine mobility, centering their weight over the leg and foot they are standing on, and softening the knee joint to create a soft, tactile relationship with the floor. As they move, they glide the soles of their feet across the surface rather than lift them into the air. Dancers learn to trust their bodies to perform reliably and spontaneously in the moment, an intuitive sensation that translates into a sense of confidence about dancing in general.

The sheer repetition of social dance proves that success is possible with a wide variety of partners, and can appear in many different forms. A dancer's sense of confidence, therefore, comes through muscle memory built through accumulated experiences of dancing. This is not so different from professional confidence coming through accumulated work experiences. But whereas a dancer's confidence is established internally, through felt sensations, as professionals we often look to build confidence externally, through documentation of our achievements. Both are useful, but only felt sensations are available to us all the time. Even in the case of remembering a past achievement, it's the triggered felt experience of the memory that refreshes our confidence, not purely the intellectual knowledge of it. Finding ways to increase awareness of our physical selves at work can make internalized confidence more accessible. Here is a list of strategies to help you build confidence more intentionally:

Body Scan: Periodically throughout the day, scan your body with your awareness, starting with your feet and moving upward through the lower legs, upper legs, hips, belly, torso, chest, arms, neck, and head. Note any sensations of tension as you sit, stand, or walk. Simply becoming aware of discomfort can begin to shift it. Permit yourself any adjustments or micro-movements to become more comfortable.

Ergonomics: When sitting, make sure your knees are below your hips, and place both feet flat on the ground. When standing, distribute your weight evenly between your two feet, and center your weight between your heels and your toes. When walking, let your arms swing naturally, and imagine your head floating lightly above your shoulders. Evaluate the ergonomics of your workstation.

Square Breathing: Used by members of the military, public speakers, and medical staff, this four-part breathing technique relaxes the nervous system and clears the mind quickly, often within seconds. Inhale for four even counts, hold your breath for four, exhale for four, and hold your breath for four again. Repeat as needed. This technique may be useful to recover from unexpected moments of high stress or before a potentially difficult meeting or conversation.

Track Record: In the face of the unknown, it's easy to forget that we've ever done anything new before. But that's never true, of course, for any of us. Recall a moment in your past in which you stepped into the unknown. Recall how you adapted, how you learned and changed as a result, and how in some way it made you the person you are today. If you have done it before, you can do it again.

Reminders: Even when we don't know what's coming, we can nevertheless choose how to show up energetically as we approach the unknown. Choose a qualitative word that represents *how* you want to feel as you perform your work. Then assign an image to represent that quality and make it easier to remember as you move through your day. There are no right or wrong answers in this exercise. Notice how your body feels as you hold the image in your mind. Consider placing a photograph, work of art, or other representation of the image on your desk or in your work space. Here are some examples of qualities and images:

Quality	Image
Confident	Redwood tree
Focused	Laser beam
Curious	Treasure map

Support System: No one succeeds alone. Write down three people, outside of work, whom you can call for support at any time. Just having the list can make you feel more confident—we say that trusted friends and colleagues *have our back*—but give yourself permission to actually call those people when you need them, too.

VULNERABILITY

On the dance floor, followers frequently accept invitations from strangers, and intentionally make themselves physically and emotionally vulnerable in the arms of their leader. The acceptance of a dance is also acceptance of a certain degree of risk. An inattentive leader may twist, squeeze, or manipulate the follower's body to cause discomfort and even injury. A distracted leader may collide with other couples, occasionally causing bodily harm. Most of the time things go well, but minor bumps and bruises are not uncommon. Dancers accept this risk, and with experience become familiar with and increasingly able to tolerate their own feelings of vulnerability. This tolerance builds bravery—the willingness to move confidently into territory before you can see it.

We may, of course, feel vulnerable at work for many different reasons. In this section, I am speaking about the vulnerability associated with creativity, especially in situations where we are asked to move beyond the limits of what we feel capable of. Depending on the nature of your work and on the quality of your professional relationships, creative problem-solving may involve different types of risk: physical, emotional, financial, social, or a combination of several or all of these. These risks, even if they seem small, can make us feel vulnerable. When we decide to express a new idea in public, or receive an unfamiliar assignment, many of us will experience a stress response. In those moments, we have two choices: shrink back or step up. There is no neutral. The more you learn to tolerate and understand your own feelings of vulnerability around creative risk-taking, the more capable you will be to serve the best interests of your team or community, and the faster you will grow personally and professionally.

In *Dare to Lead*, research professor Brené Brown defines

vulnerability as "the emotion we experience during times of uncertainty, risk, and emotional exposure."[30] Her work reveals that this feeling consistently arises around creativity and innovation. If we want to be brave, we must allow ourselves to be vulnerable. However, we need to be able to discern and interpret our own feelings of vulnerability in context. When asked to step out of the usual scope of your work or try something new, it's important to be able to determine whether the request is a stretch toward your *bravery edge* or a push against your *boundary edge.* The bravery edge usually feels a little scary but also a little exciting. You might experience it as a wish, a possibility, or an internal *yes.* There may be a sense of physical expansion or lightness.

The boundary edge, on the other hand, usually feels a little scary and a little wrong. You may experience it as an internal *no* or a sense a physical contraction, darkness, or pressure. As you increase your physical awareness and learn to read your own body's signals more clearly, these edges will become two distinct and recognizable sensations for you. They may also shift depending on the context. What was once a boundary edge may become a bravery edge, and vice versa.

PRACTICING BRAVERY

Showing up for our own creativity requires strength and focus. Often, nothing in the work environment encourages us to be more creative; we must prioritize it ourselves. The reward, however, can be tremendous. If you want your work to be a more inspiring and satisfying part of your life, these strategies may point you in the right direction.

Volunteer: In any workplace, miscellaneous tasks appear that don't fit into anyone's job description but still need to be done. Offer to take on some of these tasks, or if you see an inefficiency or a chronic speed bump in the workflow, volunteer to fix it.

---

30   Brown, *Dare to Lead*, 19.

Self-Educate: If you usually rely on someone else to answer certain questions or solve certain problems for you, learn as much as you can about these areas so that your questions or problems become less frequent and/or more precise.

Do It Anyway: It's normal to feel discomfort when we step out of our comfort zone. The feelings are not the problem; it's our interpretation of the feelings that hold us back. It's perfectly fine to feel the discomfort and do the scary thing anyway. *Note: Feelings of discomfort are also present when someone or something has pushed across a safe or ethical boundary for you. It's important to learn the difference between these two different edges in your own body: the bravery edge vs. the boundary edge. If you have reached a boundary edge, the appropriate choice would be to remain within the safe zone. See chapter 5 for more practices around maintaining healthy boundaries.*

Let It Be Imperfect: Perfectionism will rein in your bravery like nothing else will. If you're trying something new, or taking a risk of any kind, there's no way it's going to be perfect. Do your best and let it go. Chances are there will be an opportunity for you or someone else to improve on whatever it is you are doing at a later time.

Above and Beyond: Take one of your tasks or assignments to the next level by considering what larger goal it is serving. How might your task impact others in your team or organization in the future? Knowing this, what can you add or change now that would make your work more beneficial or inclusive?

Articulate a Purpose: To get clear on what inspires you to be bold and creative in your work, complete the three statements below three times each. The multiple responses will help you to get past the surface and uncover deeper insights. To what extent does your current position, team, or project align with your individual sense of purpose? What new opportunities on the horizon may allow you to align more closely with that sense of purpose?

1. *My work matters to me because* _____

1. *My work matters to me because* _____

1. *My work matters to me because* _____

2. *My work matters to my team/company because*_____

2. *My work matters to my team/company because*_____

2. *My work matters to my team/company because*_____

3. *It's worth it to perform small acts of bravery because* _____

3. *It's worth it to perform small acts of bravery because* _____

3. *It's worth it to perform small acts of bravery because* _____

WHEN OTHERS LACK VISION

Sometimes team leaders are unusually risk averse, creatively stuck, or just can't see the forest for the trees. Our bravery, in that case, usually goes unutilized. Here are some strategies to encourage imagination in others when you're feeling like things are stagnant or in a holding pattern.

New Idea: Share or develop an idea of your own in a way that is not disruptive and does not require others to take immediate action. It could be that your initiative and enthusiasm inspires some bigger thinking.

Work Small: Work within the parameters you have to make subtle improvements that keep your own creative juices flowing. You never know when one of them could grow into something larger. For example, color-code your spreadsheet, update a template, or reformat existing reference material.

Propose Solutions: Many of our jobs require frequent problem-solving. When you encounter a challenge, whether small or large, research ways to address it, or propose a few potential solutions of your own, rather than ignoring it or asking someone else to fix it.

CHAPTER 9:
INSIGHT AND STYLE

INSIGHT

+

STYLE

The Leader's Role: See potential in others
Looks Like: Identifying strengths, giving recognition and acknowledgment, expressing confidence in others, providing opportunities that match personal interests
Benefit: Accelerates innovation, inspires dedication
Impact: Inspires others to develop their strengths
When It's Missing: Missed opportunities, frustration, blind spots, low morale

---

L ike imagination in the previous chapter, insight sees what others don't yet see. But rather than dreaming into the future, insight recognizes what is already there. When we celebrate talents in others, especially if they do not easily see or value them in themselves, we help them build confidence and express those talents more fully. In *The Carrot Principle,* Adrian Gostick and Chester Elton underscore the vital importance of recognition in the workplace. They write, "It is a simple truth: we work harder at places where we feel recognized and valued for our unique contributions. And valued and engaged employees bring great value and profit to their organizations."[31] When we intentionally look for positive qualities in others, we are much more likely to see them. Once we're used to seeing them, we can develop the habit of expressing them. Everyone in the organization benefits.

The opposite, of course, is also true. When we look for deficiencies or flaws, we tend to find them. Lack of recognition results in low morale, stagnation, and disengagement. Worse, a culture of repeated criticism or punishment lowers performance and aggravates destructive patterns like perfectionism, burnout, blame, and defensiveness.

G was an executive assistant at a commercial supply company where recognition was rare. She describes the work environment as very stressful; directions from her various supervisors conflicted with one another, and workload expectations were chronically unrealistic. Among other examples of strained communication, she writes, "The feedback loop just wasn't there. Reviews were once a year, and then last year they decided to skip them. And reviews are really important. Reviews are a great time for people to say, 'Hey, how am I doing at this,' or 'Hey, I need this from you.' Reviews are a great time for people to understand 'What am I contributing? What can I contribute more of? What do I do really well?' And those were just not viewed as necessary." Of course, annual reviews are not the only opportunities to give recognition, but when we avoid even this basic tool we overlook a prime opportunity to maximize our most precious resource: our employees.

Gostick and Elton document an abundance of personal and organizational benefits produced by cultures of acknowledgment. Addressing managers and leaders, specifically, they explain, "Recognition accelerates business results. It amplifies the effect of every action and quickens every process. It also heightens your ability to see employee achievements, sharpens your communication skills,

---

31   Gostick and Elton, *The Carrot Principle*, 18–19.

creates cause for celebration, boosts trust between you and your employees, and improves accountability."[32] But giving deliberate, purposeful acknowledgment is an art form in itself, one that few of us have been trained to practice. It needs to be specific and personalized, and therefore requires something that we're not used to doing at work: getting to know one another as people. Everyone is inspired by something different. If we don't learn what those things are, we won't be able to call them forth in the professional context.

G left her job after a little over a year, citing an unhealthy work environment. In retrospect, she says, "I do know that what I did there was valued. At least, I knew that it was *valuable*. I could look at specific outcomes and make my own assessments. But I also know that they didn't want to recognize me. It just wasn't how they did things. And I want to be recognized as well as valued." This difference G points out, between objective value and recognition of that value, is a crucial one. It's the difference between the intellectual understanding of a sunset and the embodied experience of seeing one fill the evening sky with luminous streaks of color. It isn't enough to *understand* that we matter. We have to *feel* that we matter, and that feeling comes when leaders give both formal and informal recognition, and conduct personalized group celebrations. It lives in the space between us.

A VIRTUOUS CYCLE

In the introduction of this book, I described the phases of connection, collaboration, and co-creation as both progressive and cyclical. And so, every time we experience the co-creative state, the *end* becomes a new and stronger *beginning*, reinforcing the connectedness of our relationships and making even more creative work possible. This is why we develop favorite dance partners, seek

---

32   Gostick and Elton, *The Carrot Principle*, 192–193.

out the same collaborators for successive projects, or build coalitions for long-term social movements.

In the tango world, there is a rather charming tradition that conveys the couple through this transition. Social tango events are structured in sets of three-four songs. When you agree to dance with a partner, generally you agree to dance the entire set. As the couple separates in between each song, the leader traditionally gives a compliment to the follower, recognizing an admired aspect of her dancing. When given sincerely and without ulterior motive, the compliment is a potent, secret ingredient in the dance relationship. It inspires the follower to begin the *next* dance of the set with an even deeper sense of closeness, commitment, and expressiveness.

A former student of mine refers to this as "an inner call to elevate." She writes, "When a leader genuinely expresses how nice my embrace is or how nice it is to dance with me, I feel a kind of elation and realize I can let go of my inner critic. It allows me to see myself as a good partner who has her own way of dancing that other people enjoy. It helps me to relax, take more risks, and be more confident in my skills." Elder leaders claim that a heartfelt compliment calls forth a transcendent tango. In this way, the end of the co-creative moment— the last step of the dance—is marked and celebrated with an act of (re)connection, which begins the journey toward co-creation again.

In the workplace, the cycle may be harder to observe without formal rituals of acknowledgment, but it's still there. We start by cultivating trust through clear communication, inclusive practices, and expressions of care for our people. This effort promotes the flow of healthy and productive collaboration, sustainable timelines, and smooth course corrections. Finally, teams rise into the innovative, co-creative state. That state, though, is temporary by nature, and needs to dissolve back into the affirming foundation of connection so that we can rise again, perhaps more easily each time, toward co-creation. These cycles are organic and learnable. They are how we build to thrive in our work together.

The Follower's Role: Embrace who you are
Looks Like: Resourcefulness, experimentation, honoring personal interests, acting on strengths, critical thinking
Benefit: Increases self-expression
Impact: Helps others to see new possibilities
When It's Missing: Becoming bored, imitating others, comparing

The follower's view from the dance floor: *You keep pace with the rhythmic tempo of the song, and your steps fall smoothly one behind the other, the full width of the ball of your foot absorbing each beat and rolling through to touch the heel down silently: right cross, left cross, right cross, left cross. The sharpness in the music intensifies, and although your leader's signal stays the same, you add an accent to your step, mirroring the shift in the musical dynamic. Your leader responds and puts a slight delay in her signal, matching the quality in your footwork. As you turn the corner, the violin takes over the melody, and you soften your step, still landing where she directs you, but dragging your free foot in slowly as if playing the last sustained note with the edge of your shoe. Your leader responds by slowing the turn even more, then abruptly brings you to stillness as your ankles come together, suspending the moment before the next step.*

In this scene, the follower adds quality of movement to her execution of each individual step. This stylistic flair alters her timing slightly and focuses the leader's attention on specific details in the song. The resulting dialogue brings richness and complexity to the partners' combined musical interpretation, elevating the dance to a higher level of artistry.

Bravery is reaching outside your comfort zone, but style is the opposite: reaching in. What are your greatest strengths? How do you like to approach your work? Embracing and deepening these preferences reveals your own creative signature. The type of work you do doesn't matter. Software engineering, organic farming, occupational therapy—any kind of work can be done with a sense of personal style. Your job is *what* you do; your style is *how* you do it. Knowing and applying your own sense of style keeps you, your peers, and your leadership team engaged in creative and dynamic dialogue that supports not only excellent work but also outstanding work.

Remember that innovative problem-solving emerges from an environment of steady, healthy collaboration. Teams first need to be able to get the everyday nuts-and-bolts work done together smoothly. When healthy collaboration is in place, co-creativity arises organically. This chapter provides some guidance on how to facilitate that magic, but creativity is not a formula; it's more like something that occurs on its own time when you remove enough of the obstacles. In the daily flow of our work, both internal and external obstacles will always appear. The habit of clearing them away keeps the creative channel open. Like so many things, the process becomes easier and faster when we choose to lift each other up in a dance of fluid lead and follow.

MEANING

Creativity is a human quality, not something you learn at art school. No matter what you are producing or generating, whether it be digital, material, or ephemeral, you are a creator. Once we begin to look at our jobs this way, a new line of inquiry appears: *What* exactly are we creating together? Is it something we are consciously choosing? Is it something we take satisfaction in? Are we making a contribution that we deem valuable? These can be surprisingly unfamiliar questions in a hyper-capitalist society, where the primary measure of success is how much money we receive for our labor. Who cares what we're doing as long as we get paid? Sometimes it might even seem that the more we get paid, the less important it is that we enjoy what we do.

There is another way to think about work. Money is necessary to live in the world we've constructed for ourselves, and there are many useful things that can be done with it, but making it the sole criteria by which we measure our hours and our days does not result in a deep sense of meaning. On the contrary, engaging in work that is very far out of alignment with our personal values or interests can result in feelings of emptiness and dissatisfaction, and even mental and physical illness. The good news is that you don't necessarily need to change your job in order to align with your values and interests more closely. Developing a sense of personal style is one way to make your work more meaningful. If you feel restless or uninspired, start by asking yourself these questions:

1. *If I didn't have to work for money, what would I do with my life?*
Make a list. The answer(s) may surprise you.

2. *Is there anything on this list that I can scale down and act on immediately, within the parameters of my current life and work?*
You may need to miniaturize your list items. For example, if you want to travel the world, maybe you start by taking a walk at lunch. If you want to end homelessness, you might arrange to donate money or services to an organization that is doing just that.

3. *What is the one thing about my current job that I feel the most inspired by?*
Consider your field of expertise, the people you work with, your daily tasks, even your office environment or location. Anything that gives you energy counts. Focus on that thing.

INTEREST

When you've reached a level of competency in your job, it's tempting to plateau in your professional development. There are fewer incentives to refine and personalize your work beyond the stage of quality performance. And because it is uniquely yours, style cannot be defined in concrete terms; it can only be permissioned into being. Staying interested can therefore be trickier than it sounds. It requires ongoing commitment to your own sense of curiosity, discovery, and excitement. When you feel yourself just going through the motions, so to speak, how do you re-engage in your work or find new ways to approach it? How do you stay genuinely interested?

S, the physical therapist from chapter 2, told me about the immediate positive impact a specialized yoga training had on her clinic environment. This was a program that she and her colleagues enrolled in independently, not as a requirement or offering of their employer. She writes, "When thirteen PT/OT staff members took an intensive therapeutic yoga course for healthcare workers, there was a huge shift in the way we approached our therapy sessions. We incorporated breathing practices with patients and allowed for more pauses between their activities, both of which enhanced recovery. Patience and compassion expanded overall, and the whole gym was in a more peaceful state. The staff members themselves started doing more of their own self-care and yoga practice, resulting in a much happier and healthier workforce. We also held a mini yoga retreat for two other departments who had not received the training, with similar effects."

Interest is a secret back door into creativity, meaning, and purpose. In S's story, the yoga training catalyzed a new approach to work for an entire team of therapists. This new interest also materialized in an unexpected new initiative: the mini retreat. It's not necessary to seek additional training to re-engage in your work, though it may be helpful, especially if the training is in a complementary or even unrelated field.

It's the follower's task to identify what precisely provides a tangible feeling of being interested, stimulated, challenged, or curious. It will be different for each of us, and will change over time. Focus on that aspect of your work right now, and celebrate the time that you are able to devote to that thing. Perhaps, investigate whether there may be any way to spend a higher percentage of your time with activities of interest, or to let those activities influence other parts of your job.

When we approach work based on our own interests and our own intuitive ways of thinking, sensing, and communicating, managers and supervisors may begin to see possibilities in us and for us that they did not see before. They may envision the next evolution of a program, alternative applications for existing products, or new ways to refine and redefine a brand. By observing how individuals approach their work, team leaders identify original ways to further improve and develop their organizations.

IMPROVISATION

Perhaps the most distinctive feature of social dance is that it is improvised, not choreographed. Built on clear structural elements and both technical and social rules, dance improvisation nevertheless demands new and original responses to continuously changing circumstances. This paradox confounds casual onlookers as much as it bewitches devoted practitioners. How can thousands of dancers share a common vocabulary yet look so different from one another in motion? In the increasingly uncertain professional landscape, the contradiction of commonality and differentiation is a powerful way to understand team dynamics.

Improvising forces our awareness into the present, reveals new possibilities, prompts original choices, supports freedom and creativity, and inspires excellence. It trains us to be both disciplined and expressive, gracefully leveraging accumulated skills and experience to meet the challenge at hand. Following, by nature, is an expressive act, something that's easy to see in the dancer's physical movement. But our professional work, too, can be expressive if we allow it to be, and that expressiveness serves our goals in ways that only become clear when we move beyond proficiency into the realm of style.

N worked as a sales associate for a retail store, and part of her job was to set up clothing, racks, and tables according to a predesigned floor map. After working at the store for some time, she made some small changes to the floor map. She recalls, "I really enjoy the visual design aspect of retail, and I just wanted to try something different." Changing the plan could have felt risky or wrong, but N chose to trust her own aesthetic sense and stay in the moment, focusing on the *how* of her task, rather than the *what*. When her supervisor noticed the changes a few days later, she was pleasantly surprised and gave N leeway to experiment further. Of course, the supervisor could have had the opposite reaction, but N took a calculated risk, adding small personal adjustments to an existing structure. What could have remained a monotonous daily task became an opportunity to express her artistic sensibility and improve the presentation of the store.

On the level of felt experience, the most connected, collaborative, and co-creative dance couples seem to collapse lead and follow roles into one. Many dancers describe a fluid experience of not knowing who is leading or who is following, of effortlessly moving together through space, of mutual surprise and discovery. In truly creative professional teams, a similar phenomenon takes place. When groups are at their most integrated, their most creative, it isn't always so clear who is leading and who is following. It doesn't seem to matter. Really great following feels like leading, and really great leading feels like following. If we are closely connected to our colleagues, both up and down the hierarchy, this odd reversal is seamless and imperceptible. We don't notice what's happening because what's happening is serving the shared goal far better than anyone could have predicted. Was N following when she made those changes to the floor plan? Or was she leading? How about her supervisor? If there is fluid dialogue, it doesn't matter. This is the alchemy of lead and follow in action.

We may strive to inhabit a co-creative state as much as possible, but in reality, we can't be there all the time, and we can't always predict when it will arise. What we *can* do is cultivate the conditions that make the seamless experience more likely, which is exactly what social dancers do. They do it in a way that may seem counterintuitive, by consciously differentiating the leading and following roles in both education and practice. By differentiating, though, dancers achieve the merging of those same roles in their actual lived experience: the co-creative paradox.

Many teams and organizations miss out on the benefits of the co-creative phenomenon because they fail to acknowledge the essential interplay of leading and following in the first place. Before leading and following can dissolve into fluid collaboration, they must each be able to stand on their own. What dancers call *improvisation* is a high art form. It requires strong conviction in one another's human potential and a shared embrace of the unknown. It is through improvising, or collaborating, for countless hours that dancers develop their own style, and so it is for all of us in our work as well.

When you work in relationship with many other people, you won't always know *what* you'll be doing next, but you can nevertheless invest yourself in the *how* of doing it. That is, you can guide yourself more by your own values and taste than by what others may have done before you, or by so-called conventional wisdom. You can avoid comparison and seek personal excellence instead. You can make the dance your own.

PRACTICING STYLE

The day-to-day activity of work can be tiring and repetitive, and maintaining a personal investment in mundane tasks can get tricky over time. You want to be creative and to enjoy your work, but it doesn't always seem attainable. One way to get there is to identify exactly what creativity *feels like* for you, independent of your job description and separate from any one favorite hobby or artistic practice. Once you connect to your own creative energy in a more general way, and on a regular basis, your approach to work may shift on its own. Here are some suggestions:

Pleasure: You can stimulate creative energy indirectly by doing something you enjoy, like taking a walk outdoors or eating something delicious for lunch.

Artwork: Hang some original art in your work space. It can be art made by anyone: your two-year-old niece, a friend, yourself, or a professional artist. Art stimulates the right brain. Having some in your work space can elevate your mood and make you feel more engaged. Choose art that you genuinely love. Add or rotate in a new piece once a quarter or once a year.

Nature: A generous and visceral reminder of the eternal process of growth and change, the natural environment embodies the creative process. Keep a potted plant or cut flowers on your desk, or simply observe the trees, plants, and grasses that peek through our towns and cities.

Novelty: Read a novel, bake a cake, take a dance lesson. Do something new for the sake of doing something new, and be open to the experience.

Organize: The seemingly mundane act of desk or office organization can be a practical way of boosting your creative energy. The trick is choosing to see this as a creative challenge rather than an unpleasant chore or a vehicle for procrastination. Incorporate a variety of physical movements like lifting, reaching, crouching, and carrying to make the impact even greater.

Advocate: Speak up about things that are important to you. If you see an opportunity for your team or organization to align more fully with a cultural value or social cause, propose or suggest a way to do so. Gather support for it from your coworkers.

WHEN OTHERS OVERLOOK YOU

Managers are constantly juggling tasks and coordinating multiple streams of work, including their own. They can't always see the details, or track something as subtle as your personal level of creative flow. You can help by showing it to them in clear and non-distracting ways. Here are some ideas:

Fix It: Identify a chronic problem that everyone complains about, and come up with a solution for it. If you can, implement the solution on your own.

Express Interest: As simple as it may sound, stating your interest in a specific type of work or an upcoming project may be all it takes for the opportunity to be offered to you.

Refresh: Improve the formatting on resource files, add additional detail to a design, or ask yourself what might be missing from an existing project. Offering small added values might draw your leader's attention to your gifts.

Track Accomplishments: A good career-building practice in itself, maintaining a list of your own past accomplishments, particularly the creative ones, keeps them fresh in your mind so that you can refer to them when discussing future projects or negotiating the distribution of work tasks. If you know what you love and what you're good at, offer to do more of the same.

AFTERWORD

Many wisdom traditions teach that as we accept ourselves more fully, we are able to enjoy more authentic relationships with others. I hope this book has reinforced that truth, and also illuminated a complementary one: that by learning to relate to others more intentionally, we are better able to embrace ourselves as complex, holistic individuals. Tango presents an elegant model for the interplay of leadership and followership—one portal through which to step into our own complexity and wholeness as employees, advocates, collaborators, and citizens of a changing world.

Perhaps you are becoming more curious about harmonizing leadership and followership within yourself. Or maybe you're wondering whether it's really practical to stand in the leader's shoes one moment and in the follower's shoes the next. Choreographer Valeria Solomonoff's *Solo Duet* presents a compelling image of just such a character. Premiered in 2002 in NYC, her three-minute tango splices together the postural affects, gestures, and footwork of the archetypal leader with those of the archetypal follower. Alternating between facing back and facing front, stretching out her arms one moment and dropping into a deep lunge the next, the performer contains a complete tango conversation within a single body. More than simply an inventive fantasy, I see the nimble pantsuited character of *Solo Duet* as a kind of lead-and-follow prototype. In both her costume and her affect, she combines the complementary strengths of both masculine and feminine roles without dissolving or neutralizing either. What better way to fashion ourselves as dynamic professional agents?

Yet, I feel an echo of loneliness in the steps of this tango, the clench of stamina it takes to contain the dialogue within a single body rather than volleying it back and forth with others. The contradiction of Solomonoff's title—*Solo Duet*—reminds me of the many hours I spend sitting alone at the screen, cycling through the many well-worn hats that self-employed folks inevitably wear, leading and following myself. Likewise, the choreographer herself tells me, "I made this piece out of necessity, because I didn't have a partner." The character of *Solo Duet* is not a soloist by choice, but by circumstance.

As much as I treasure the freedom and flexibility of my independent work, I also feel its inherent tenuousness and fragility. Watching the ranks of my fellow gig workers grow, I'm more and more aware of the need to consciously build community around myself, professional and otherwise. And that is when I remember that community building is actually baked into the practice of tango social dance. The common phrase "It takes two to tango" is deceptive, if not flat-out wrong. Social dancers don't pair off in isolation; they dance in restaurants, bars, and event halls full of other people, mixing and matching amongst themselves throughout the evening. Music is curated by a DJ or performed by a live orchestra. On the dance floor, the uncertainty of other couples' movements make pre-planning impossible. At the same time, there is a certain ease and comfort in taking one's place in the flow of the *ronda*—the reliable counterclockwise movement of dancers around the floor. This community aspect of the tradition is what brings dancers into the present moment in the first place, and what makes it safe to explore the fertile territory of the unknown as leaders and followers. It may take two to tango, but it takes a village to dance.

I'm finishing this book in late 2020, a year in which the COVID-19 pandemic, widespread civil unrest, and unprecedented climate crises forced a national reckoning with social justice, economic sustainability, and democracy itself. I urge us to keep these conversations alive as we navigate both our professional careers and our personal trajectories over the next generation and beyond; they require focused attention and creative energy. In seeking healthy, sustainable solutions, we have an opportunity to reimagine not only *what* we are doing, but also *how* and *why* we are doing it at every level. The process guides the product as much as the other way around. If we want a truly equitable and just society, we must embody the values of equity and justice every day as we work together, no matter what that *work* happens to be. Practicing leadership and followership as complementary creative forces is one way of shifting ourselves toward balance. Every conversation is improvised in the moment, and it is in the moment where all possibilities exist.

Reclaiming followership is key because history proves that tectonic cultural shifts rarely begin at the top, though ultimately leaders must be involved. Rather, change is historically initiated from the bottom—the *grassroots*. Bottom-up movement is the direction of followership, with its distinctive character of responsiveness. We cannot wait for individual leaders to direct us, nor for existing systems of leadership to change. Rather, we must activate followership within ourselves and within our communities, engaging the aspect of our power that flows upward, lifting and supporting ourselves and others. So activated, we can engage more effectively with those we permit to lead us, providing the perspective and accountability they need to connect, collaborate, and co-create with us in transforming organizations and institutions from the inside out. May this way of thinking about teamwork inspire you to step into this evolving moment as dancers do: with confidence, grace, and an enduring curiosity for what comes next.

ACKNOWLEDGMENTS

Deepest gratitude to Ira Chaleff, mentor and friend, and pioneer of courageous followership. The mysterious hand of fate guided Ira into one of my tango classes in 2008. He not only encouraged me to write about followership through a tango dancer's lens, but also gently guided me through the process of thinking, feeling, and doing that writing over the next decade. This book is inspired by his work, and would not exist without him.

If *Lead & Follow* would not exist without Ira, it would not be what it is without the powerful influence of coach and teacher Amy Lombardo. Many of the practices and inquiry questions in these pages were inspired by the sensitive and pragmatic training I received from her. Amy believed in this book when it was still in seed form, advised on its structure, and helped me hold the vision for it.

Enormous thanks to my early readers, my adventurous pilot testers, and all those who provided the personal stories that bring leadership and followership to life in these pages. Your feedback and experiences sharpened the details, informed key additions and subtractions, and made this book a thousand times stronger. I am so grateful to have had so many wonderful and inspiring conversations with you and hope to have many more.

Special shout-out to every last member of the global tango community, past and present. The source material for this book was gathered over many years while walking those miles around and around the *ronda*. By loving tango, you have sustained the world in which I learned everything that I know about leadership and followership. I hope this book makes you proud to be a dancer, and to carry the deep wisdom of tango in your body.

And finally, my most profound thanks to Isaac for dancing with me through this life, for getting excited about this book and never doubting it would materialize, for being a tireless sounding board, and for supporting me and being an incredible partner in every way possible. Every single day I wake up grateful for you and for us.

JOURNAL

This journal is provided as a guide to track your own discoveries as you work through the material in this book, either on your own or as part of a group. I suggest spending one to two weeks on each chapter. Please choose a pace that works well for you.

CHAPTER 1: CLARITY AND ATTENTION

1. The practice(s) I tried:

2. When, where, or with whom I tried them:

3. What I observed as a result of the practice:

4. What I plan to start doing (or stop doing) from now on:

5. What I plan to do more of (or less of) from now on:

6. How this chapter informs my understanding of leadership and followership:

CHAPTER 2: INCLUSION AND ENGAGEMENT

1. The practice(s) I tried:

2. When, where, or with whom I tried them:

3. What I observed as a result of the practice:

4. What I plan to start doing (or stop doing) from now on:

5. What I plan to do more of (or less of) from now on:

6. How this chapter informs my understanding of leadership and followership:

CHAPTER 3: CARE AND OPENNESS

1. The practice(s) I tried:

2. When, where, or with whom I tried them:

3. What I observed as a result of the practice:

4. What I plan to start doing (or stop doing) from now on:

5. What I plan to do more of (or less of) from now on:

6. How this chapter informs my understanding of teamwork:

CHAPTER 4: STRUCTURE AND DELIVERY

1. The practice(s) I tried:

2. When, where, or with whom I tried them:

3. What I observed as a result of the practice:

4. What I plan to start doing (or stop doing) from now on:

5. What I plan to do more of (or less of) from now on:

6. How this chapter informs my understanding of teamwork:

CHAPTER 5: EXPECTATIONS AND BOUNDARIES

1. The practice(s) I tried:

2. When, where, or with whom I tried them:

3. What I observed as a result of the practice:

4. What I plan to start doing (or stop doing) from now on:

5. What I plan to do more of (or less of) from now on:

6. How this chapter informs my understanding of teamwork:

CHAPTER 6: ADAPTABILITY AND FLEXIBILITY

1. The practice(s) I tried:

2. When, where, or with whom I tried them:

3. What I observed as a result of the practice:

4. What I plan to start doing (or stop doing) from now on:

5. What I plan to do more of (or less of) from now on:

6. How this chapter informs my understanding of teamwork:

CHAPTER 7: DECISIVENESS AND PRESENCE

1. The practice(s) I tried:

2. When, where, or with whom I tried them:

3. What I observed as a result of the practice:

4. What I plan to start doing (or stop doing) from now on:

5. What I plan to do more of (or less of) from now on:

6. How this chapter informs my understanding of teamwork:

CHAPTER 8: IMAGINATION AND BRAVERY

1. The practice(s) I tried:

2. When, where, or with whom I tried them:

3. What I observed as a result of the practice:

4. What I plan to start doing (or stop doing) from now on:

5. What I plan to do more of (or less of) from now on:

6. How this chapter informs my understanding of teamwork:

CHAPTER 9: INSIGHT AND STYLE

1. The practice(s) I tried:

2. When, where, or with whom I tried them:

3. What I observed as a result of the practice:

4. What I plan to start doing (or stop doing) from now on:

5. What I plan to do more of (or less of) from now on:

6. How this chapter informs my understanding of teamwork:

SUMMARY

Look back through your journal notes to gather your takeaways and go-to strategies for teamwork going forward. The questions below will help you integrate these new practices into your work life:

1. Which of the leadership and/or followership skills described in this book feel the most comfortable for you? Which ones feel the most challenging? Why do you think that is the case?

2. What do you observe about yourself when you're in the leadership role? The followership role? Where does each role serve you best in your current job?

3. How might stronger leadership and/or followership skills make you more successful individually? Which skills seem most important to focus on right now?

4. How might stronger leadership and/or followership skills make your team more successful overall? Which skills seem most important to focus on right now?

5. Write down one specific goal that you'd like to achieve within the next year. How will you use both leadership and followership skills to move toward that goal?

BIBLIOGRAPHY

Allen, David. *Getting Things Done: The Art of Stress-Free Productivity.* rev. ed. New York: Penguin, 2015.

Brown, Brené. *Dare to Lead: Brave Work. Tough Conversations. Whole Hearts,* New York: Random House, 2018.

———. *Daring Greatly: How the Courage to Be Vulnerable Transforms the Way We Live, Love, Parent, and Lead.* New York: Avery, 2012

Chaleff, Ira. *The Courageous Follower: Standing up to and for our Leaders.* 3rd ed. San Francisco: Berrett-Koehler Publishers, 2009.

———. *Intelligent Disobedience: Doing Right When What You're Told to Do Is Wrong.* San Francisco: Berrett-Koehler Publishers, 2015.

Edmondson, Amy. *The Fearless Organization: Creating Psychological Safety in the Workplace for Learning, Innovation, and Growth.* Hoboken: John Wiley & Sons, 2018.

Einstein, Albert. *Einstein on Cosmic Religion and Other Opinions and Aphorisms.* New York: Dover, 2009

Goleman, Daniel. *Emotional Intelligence: Why it can Matter More than IQ.* New York: Bantam Books, 1995.

Gostick, Adrian, and Chester Elton. *The Carrot Principle: How the Best Managers Use Recognition to Engage Their Employees, Retain Talent, and Drive Performance.* New York: Free Press, 2007.

Hurwitz, Marc, and Samantha Hurwitz. *Leadership is Half the Story: A Fresh Look at Followership, Leadership, and Collaboration.* Toronto: University of Toronto Press, 2015.

Kellerman, Barbara. *The End of Leadership.* New York: Harper Business, 2012.

Kelley, Robert E. *The Power of Followership: How to Create Leaders People Want to Follow and Followers Who Lead Themselves.* New York: Currency Doubleday, 1992

———. "Rethinking Followership," In *The Art of Followership: How Great Followers Create Great Leaders and Organizations*, edited by Ron Riggio, Ira Chaleff, and Jean Lipman-Blumen, 5-15. San Francisco: Jossey-Bass, 2008.

Lombardo, Amy. *Brilliance: A Coaching Guide to Clearing Inner Obstacles and Letting Your Authenticity Shine.* Life Tree Media, 2019.

Margolis, Michael. *Story 10X: Turn the Impossible into the Inevitable.* Storied, 2019.

Robbins, Mike. *Bring Your Whole Self to Work: How Vulnerability Unlocks Creativity, Connection, and Performance.* Carlsbad: Hay House, 2018.

Voss, Chris. *Never Split the Difference: Negotiating As If Your Life Depended On It.* New York: HarperCollins, 2016.

Shenk, Joshua Wolf. *Powers of Two: Finding the Essence of Innovation in Creative Pairs.* New York: Houghton Mifflin, 2014.

Zak, Paul. *The Trust Factor: The Science of Creating High-Performance Companies.* New York: AMACOM, 2017.

CPSIA information can be obtained
at www.ICGtesting.com
Printed in the USA
LVHW030254050221
678442LV00007B/379